SURVIVAL TACTICS

SURVIVAL TACTICS

How to Make Profits in Difficult Times

John Yates

MERCURY

First published in 1992
by Mercury Books
Gold Arrow Publications Limited,
862 Garratt Lane, London SW17 0NB

Set in Palatino by TecSet Ltd.
Printed and bound in Great Britain by
Mackays of Chatham plc, Chatham, Kent

British Library Cataloguing in Publication Data

Disclaimer: No responsibility for loss occasioned to any person acting or
refraining from action as a result of any material in this publication can be
accepted by the author or publisher.

ISBN 1–85251–136–2

CONTENTS

Acknowledgements   vi

1 Survival is not compulsory   1

2 The making of profit   6

3 Survival strategy   13

4 Forty potential areas of cost reduction   19

5 Twenty-five ways to increase revenue   66

6 Popular ways to put up profits   86

7 Recession tactics   89

8 DIY profit protection programme   108

9 Conclusion   115

   Appendix: Check-list for increased profit   117

   Bibliography   125

   Index   127

ACKNOWLEDGEMENTS

This book owes much to the written and spoken thoughts of better minds, and the generosity of business friends, clients, and colleagues, in their sharing of the good (and bad) ways of running businesses. In some ways it is harder to talk about our failures than our successes and, as some of the examples I have used might be candidates for the literal version of 'It'll be all right on the night', I thank the companies concerned.

Thanks are also due to Ian Harty, Paul Bennetts, Chris Holleran, and John Boulter for their specific contributions on how to do things well.

I am grateful to Tina Ellison who made sense and sentences out of my scribblings.

1

SURVIVAL IS NOT COMPULSORY

To gain wealth is easy; to keep it, hard.

Chinese proverb

The title of this chapter, *Survival is not Compulsory,* is one-half of a quotation from arguably the most important post-war quality control pioneer, Dr W. Edwards Deming. The full quotation is a classic piece of understatement: 'There is no need to do this. Survival is not compulsory.' Deming is referring here to the systematic, rigorous approach to problem-solving which is his trademark. He says that the adoption of an action plan is necessary if managements intend to stay in business and protect investors and jobs.

This book contains ideas to keep the gap between price and cost as wide as possible, which are not new, but restatements of common-sense methods, tried and tested. Its purpose is to act as an *aide mémoire* for companies who need to protect the profit margin in a hostile business climate.

In the world of business there is no surer way of protecting profits than through better control of internal expenses. It is the one opportunity area which is available to management regardless of the difficulties of the market-place. I have spoken to executives of profitable companies over the years in order to try to find an answer to the question of what makes a company successful. Regardless of the business they are in or any particular marketing or product advantage, the thing they have in common is the detailed control they exercise over what is happening in the business.

In 1982, while helping a public limited company in the printing industry improve profits by a better cost-estimating

1

routine, I was surprised by the degree of cost detail involved and the use of figures to one tenth part of a penny. The chairman defended the practice with the words, 'Many a mickle makes a muckle' (English translation, 'Much of a little makes a lot'). That approach underlines the main thrust of this book. Although companies may realize profit improvement from one single new idea, widening the gap between revenue and expenditure is achievable mainly by attention to small details of business in areas which should be under control.

Former UK Prime Minister, Ted Heath, was haunted by a remark he was supposed to have made that his Government would 'at a stroke, reduce the rise in prices, increase productivity, and reduce unemployment'. That is not an easy thing to achieve, as he found out. The way to reduce costs, increase profit, and maintain people in jobs is by attention to a hundred little everyday things.

Figure 1 is a simple representation of the aim of all companies – to optimize profit – and the need for detailed control. Companies budget to produce optimum profit, but profit evaporates as additional overheads and manufacturing costs are incurred or companies fail to achieve budgeted sales volume or prices. These reductions in profit are like leaks in a bucket: budgeted profits will run away if managers do not pay enough attention to the causes.

How small a reduction in costs is needed to make substantial contributions to profit is illustrated by a list published in 1990 in

Figure 1 Profit evaporation through lack of control

Revenue:	★★★★★★	
less Cost of sales:	★	This forms the budget, the
less Necessary overheads:	★	management plan of action.
= Optimum profit:	★★★★	
less Unnecessary overheads:	★	
less Excess cost of sales:	★	Profit evaporation occurs
less Price erosion:	★	when we are not in control.
= Actual profit:	★	

the magazine *Management Today*, which showed the relative increase in profit for each percentage cut in materials or wages. For example, a cut of 10 per cent in the wage bill of British Aerospace would increase pre-tax profit by over 60 per cent. At ASDA, a 10 per cent cut in material costs would increase profit by 84 per cent, while a 10 per cent cut in materials at ICI would achieve 57 per cent better profits.

As every sixth-form economics student knows, there are only two ways to increase profits: raise revenue or reduce costs. In a typical company the cost-reduction method has a sharper impact on profit improvement than the volume-increase method. Every pound saved will improve the profit figure by £1, whereas it is likely that increases in sales of some £20 will be required to increase profitability by £1. The effect of small cost savings on overall profits is further shown in Table 1,

Table 1 The effect of cost savings on profits

	Column 1	Column 2	Column 3
	Year 1	Year 2	Managed Change, Year 2
Sales	100	90	90
Materials	45	40.5	38.48 (−5%)
Labour	15	13.5	12.83 (−5%)
Overheads	30	30.0	27.00 (−10%)
Profit	10	6	11.7

Notes
Column 1 shows that for every £100 of sales the net profit is £10.
Column 2 assumes that, in a difficult year, sales revenue drops by 10 per cent. It further assumes that prime material and labour costs are so controlled that they are cut in proportion to the decline in revenue (i.e., 10 per cent). It also assumes that the company does not reduce its overheads: (*a*) partly because it cannot react quickly enough; (*b*) partly because some of them are fixed; and (*c*) partly because management is not in control of them. The result is that the 10 per cent sales reduction will produce only 60 per cent of the Year 1 profit level. Column 3 shows that if the company manages internal costs by being only 5 per cent more efficient with labour and material, and reduces its overhead proportional to the change in turnover (10 per cent), it could end the year with profits which are greater than Year 1!

which illustrates the experience of a typical manufacturing company.

It is appropriate, therefore, that this book devotes more space to cost-reduction ideas than sales improvement, although the revenue-raising avenue to profit increases is addressed in Chapter 5.

You will find in this book references to recession and survival. As trade fluctuates cyclically there will be, inevitably, a low point of business – 'a recession' – as the UK has experienced about every ten years over the past thirty. The ideas of cost reduction and revenue increase, however, are just as applicable in good times as in bad. In boom years profits are easier to find and managers have less incentive to work hard at optimizing them, yet these are the years when maximum profits should be contributing to the build-up of good reserves for the next downturn.

Many of the ideas for profit improvement are simple and even mundane, but the examples should serve to illustrate the quantum effect which relatively small cost reductions can have on the profit margin. These improvements depend on management's ability to 'mind the shop' better, to pay close attention to cost details, and to control what goes on in the business. Spring Ram plc, for example, in little over ten years has become the largest manufacturer of synthetic bathroom and kitchen furniture in the UK, with 25 per cent of the UK bath market, 15 per cent of the flat-pack kitchens, and 12 per cent of the loos and basins. It raced to a £60m turnover in its first eight years, and to £145m by year eleven with £30m profits. Bill Rooney, its chairman, plays down the success: 'It's been easy getting to where we are. There's no secret formula, just boring, common-sense management.'

This book does not offer a panacea, no new management action or single new technique guaranteed to snatch success from the jaws of failure. It contains no flash of inspiration, no revelation of a new truth. It is a relisting of the basic but important things which management does in a profitable business.

It is not a book for the long haul. It will fail as a management creed, except in the sense that thrift is a desirable characteristic. It has no pretence to replace long-term strategic planning, nor to advise against research and development projects which have long gestation periods.

It offers short-term solutions to chronic problems of today. This 'today' can be the now of a recession; or the now of a downturn in a particular industry; or the threat from a single new competitor or new environmental legislation. To imply as we do here that managers should 'stick to the knitting' in difficult times can only be a short-term policy, because eventually companies must be prepared to change and adapt – or go out of business.

> *The essence of excellence is the thousand concrete, minute actions performed by everyone ... to keep a company on course.*
>
> Tom Peters, *The Pursuit of Excellence*

2

THE MAKING OF PROFIT

It is a socialist idea that making profits is a vice. I consider the real vice is making losses.

Winston Churchill

As a non-accountant, I have often been intrigued by the way in which profit is perceived in business. To read the aims of some companies, it is the objective of all our efforts, like Marks & Spencer whose aim is 'to make a profit and serve the community' and Jaguar Cars whose aim is 'to make money by satisfying customers'.

The way in which management addresses profit is interesting. In a company organizational structure we see people with specific responsibility for sales, production, research and development, accounts, quality, personnel, training, transport, pensions, and so on, but no one with designated responsibility for profit. Yet this, the purpose of all our efforts, is too important to be left as a by-product of all other activities, the remnants of income when all cost centres have taken their fill.

One might say that the managing director is responsible for profit – but the MD is responsible for everything, and if the captain of the ship is busy stoking the boiler, who does the steering? Others with likely responsibility for profit include the finance director or the cost accountant. Yet the former in most companies has a role which measures where the company has been and how it has done, while the latter is usually a reporter on profit without the responsibility for making it happen.

I suppose that part of the problem is caused by the way we treat profit in the book-keeping sense. It is what is left at the bottom of the profit and loss account, yet it has specific purposes just as important as, say, depreciation, capital purchases, directors' bonus, bank loan repayments, and other items above the line; indeed, it is the funds for these in the future. We isolate profit in this singularly peculiar way for fiscal reasons – because companies are taxed on it and government dues are based on what that bottom figure says. A lot of management initiative is even spent on finding ways of keeping much of the income out of the profit figure. Taxes have been with us for over four thousand years, and we live with them, but it does not mean that we have to look at the way we control our businesses through tax-tinted glasses. If there were still a tax on windows, would we brick them all up and work in the dark?

Profit is a generic label which can blur the separate purposes for the surplus of income over expenditure, such as funds for capital purchases, research and development, repayment to shareholders, contingency cash for a rainy day. Why not, therefore, appoint a Profit Manager, someone responsible for dealing with the profitable portion of revenue as determined by the budget? Why not take the 15 per cent or 20 per cent forecast net profit out of every cheque received and deposit this in a profit account, and then make managers manage the other areas of expenditure with what is left? When Gareth Davies, head of Glynwed International, was the group financial director in the 1970s, he required all the companies in the group to give head office 25 per cent of all their assets in cash – every year.

Why not, for internal management purposes, account for future investment, dividends, capital expenditure, and so forth, above the line? What about swapping profit with directors' bonus in the profit and loss account? In the budget, why not determine the level of surplus required for the above future purposes and let any remainder *after that* be distributed as bonuses? One of the additional advantages which such a calculation would have is that the 'shyness' which has for years prevented UK management from sharing the company accounts with the workforce could be overcome. The bottom line would then be truly surplus and could be distributed as bonuses, to everyone! How much easier to talk to employees and trade unions about that kind of trading account. More

7

importantly, instead of profit being whatever is left on the plate, it becomes the ingredients for another meal on another day.

Profit control

Unless you are one of those people who believe that all will be well if you stick your head in the sand, then you will know that a profitable company is best assured by pro-active business management. In a survey carried out after the recession of the early 1980s, creditors of companies which had gone out of business put poor management as the principal cause of the business failure. In the nature of assessing risk when bank managers and venture capitalists are asked to provide investment funds, the single most important element in the decision-making process is the assessment of the quality of management. I once heard a venture capitalist list the top ten important things in determining the quality of risk; eight of the ten were management characteristics.

I must have met thousands of senior managers, directors, and owners of UK businesses, and the one visible common denominator in the good ones is the knowledge they have about what is going on in the business. Poor managers hesitate or give vague answers when asked about even simple business indicators like profit margins, indebtedness, liquidity, or order book. The best managers *know*.

Why do we need controls

Controls should provide essential management information so that managers can do just that – manage. We have all seen small businesses work very well and very profitably without control systems, but this is because the owner/manager is so close to what is happening in the company that he knows exactly what is going on. It is impossible for executives of larger companies to have this same degree of sensitivity about the business, or for managers of different departments in larger companies to know how best to play their part in the company's operations, without good management controls.

The better the control applied, the more potential weaknesses will be highlighted, anticipated, and overcome. In larger companies the control must necessarily be detailed, as each part must be controlled in order to manage the whole. The benefits of control are manifold and different in each company situation but they include:

- better planning;
- increased commitment;
- improved motivation;
- better decision-making;
- economic use of time;
- improved efficiency;
- improved competitive edge;
- and most importantly – more profit.

A BIM survey published in 1986 on manufacturing operations in the UK was able to compare companies with control systems on, for example, delivery performance, with those companies who had no formal monitoring systems. On the simple criterion of 'only one order in four late', nearly 70 per cent of plants with good control systems hit this target, but only 31 per cent of plants without monitoring systems achieved even this level of delivery performance.

Are you in control?

I have heard managers admit their lack of control without being unduly concerned about improving it. In difficult trading times profit retention *is* possible by controlling internal costs, but improved control is possible only through improved information. Up-to-date and accurate information not only tells what has happened but is the means by which management can anticipate change trends.

It is not sufficient to believe that because we were in control last year or last month or last week that we are still in control.

Change is endemic in industry as in life. We may think that we work in the same market place, with the same people, for the same customers, but we don't! Change is the one constant element. As the philosopher Heraclitus said, 'It is not possible to step twice into the same river.'

Regular and frequent reports mean fewer surprises about the state of the company. Firms with only annual accounts have one chance a year to measure the company's viability; with monthly reports there are twelve opportunities to see if anything is wrong. In some situations it will be appropriate to have weekly or even daily reports. So in the protection of profits the need is for vigilance. That is why companies need good reporting systems and why managers need to pay attention to what the reports are telling them.

A survey carried out by CBI/PA into UK productivity in 1988 showed that half of all staff and at least a quarter of all management do not receive regular information on the productivity performance of their department or company. If the information needed for good control is not made available in a routine way then management does not have the means of control. Not only are managers not in possession of important facts, but they may be wasting time reading the information which is produced and other people's time in producing it. The better the control of information, the better the chances of detecting situations which need management attention and the more which can be done to improve profitability.

Just-in-time experts use the illustration of the company as a ship floating on a sea of raw material and components. As management try to reduce the stocks of material and parts, the level of water reduces and rocks appear in the form of bottlenecks, hold-ups, plant breakdowns, and so on, which endanger the ship. The philosophy of improvement must not be to keep stocks high to avoid the rocks, but to lower them as far as possible and to eliminate the problem rocks as they appear. Good management controls are like sonar and radar which define the impediments to company progress and anticipate problems which can then be overcome.

Measurement provides the means of control

Why do companies comparable in size and even in the same business generate vastly different profit levels? They might be constrained by market forces to set similar prices for their products, yet one company will produce significantly better margins than the other. The reason often lies in the management and control of resources like people, materials, overheads, space, and the like. Control requires knowledge and measurement, and the use of information which is commonly available to turn companies which struggle to be profitable into secure and flourishing enterprises. If management knows what is going on it will be in a position to make things happen, and managers who control events run profitable companies.

Barclays Bank has started measuring staff productivity in its 2600 branches for the first time, as it and other clearing banks embark on programmes of job loss and restructuring to reduce costs. The bank has devised a measure of productivity based on the cost of staff in each branch against twenty-nine output measures, including cash paid out, how many savings accounts are opened, and the number of admitted standing orders processed.

Let me give an example of cost-reduction possibilities when information is widely available, this time in a non-industrial situation. The regional water authority for the Isle of Wight has issued meters to residents as a trial exercise for metering all households. The reduction in the amount of water used has been so dramatic that in the summer of 1990, while the rest of southern England was under a water restriction, including a hose-pipe ban, Isle of Wight residents had no such restrictions.

Control requires the necessary production of indicators of business activity in sales, purchasing, production, inventory, finance, people, and markets. If managers can enumerate activity in a non-subjective way, replacing gut feeling or instinct with reliable information, they can ask important business questions in the confidence that answers are meaningful and will contribute to correct management decisions.

In twenty years in management consultancy, I have not ceased to be surprised at owners and managers who are content with low profit margins. In a recent survey of small and

11

medium-sized companies, the net profit before tax ranged from 2 per cent to 11 per cent of turnover. It is the aim of this book to show how to improve such figures.

Some company managers appear to be unaware of the profit-draining cost of running a company. Many overhead costs are small and considered not reducible because they appear to be fixed. Because they are small, they are often ignored as potential sources of profit evaporation. Yet it is the constant nature of these costs which makes them important; the accumulation of these small costs can offset profits just as surely as the large and more obvious cost centres.

One important need in the control of a company is adequate, up-to-date, comprehensive, and timely information on all significant cost centres, in sufficient detail to enable management to take considered action. This book will repeatedly emphasize the importance of generating and using such information. Take a look at what other companies do, and try to match or improve on the best. Inmac, the computer and datacomm equipment suppliers, has ninety staff at its East Kilbride factory but only five managers! The general manager, Alan Richardson, is quoted as saying, 'Once the controls are there, the routine will run OK.'

During the 1990–1 recession, the chairman of Caparo Industries, Swraj Paul, initiated a monthly circular to his senior managers headed, 'Think Lean – Act Mean', epitomizing 'the spirit we have to bring to bear upon all aspects of our work. We are having, unfortunately, to remember and in some cases relearn all those cost-saving and working capital reduction techniques we lived with during the early 1980s.'

H.J. Heinz has doubled sales and trebled profits over the past decade, yet never diversified outside the food business.

I believe that the three most important words in difficult times are these: control, control, control. When times are difficult stay with what you know best. Stay in control, stay lean and stay profitable.

If everyone stuck to his talent, the cows would be well tended.

J.P. De Florian

3

SURVIVAL STRATEGY

A businessman is judged by the company he keeps solvent.
                                          Herbert V.Prochnon

Like the answer from the village yokel to the request for the directions to a remote rural location, 'If I wur goin' thur I wudn' start from here', survival in bad times should really start in the good times! To everything there is a season, and trade is no exception. The post-war UK economic cycles have turned full circle every ten years or so, and management should recognize that each decade will carry some very poor years.

In the 1991 recession, the UK truck market fell by half. While other companies worried about a cut-back in production and jobs, ERF took it all in its stride; the company had lots of cash, and management was able to look beyond the recession and plan for the upturn. In the 1980 recession, however, the company nearly went bankrupt and were saved only by understanding bankers. Its product range was chaotic and its production processes were inefficient. Ten years later the management could be relaxed about the downturn because, ahead of the recession in 1991, ERF's board started to reduce production in expectation of a downturn. In the good years ERF had produced a more standardized truck range and cut the number of in-house operations. Now they have no huge machine shops and foundries; all they do is turn off the tap from the suppliers.

Companies with assets, whether liquid or otherwise, survive best in lean times. If liquid, there is a competitive edge from using the company's own money, not the bank's. If not liquid, like land or property or investments, there is little difficulty in

13

obtaining funds to support the company. I have observed at first hand the difference such collateral makes. Two companies with similar-sized businesses in terms of turnover and staff, one of which, with land and buildings as security, has an overdraft facility of £280 000 and has been offered more by the local bank manager; the other, without the necessary security and with a facility of £120 000, could not even raise a further £5000.

Using the good times to lay down reserves will provide freedom to explore options in a recession, and to take the necessary management action to suit the company, not the bank.

Short-term targets

When the hard times come, think short term. Assuming that you know which products and/or activities are profitable (if you don't, then find out), begin to cut out those which do not contribute to profits. This you can do by knowing true costs, evaluating the best selling price which can be obtained, and determining whether you can reduce costs in order to produce an acceptable profit margin. If it is still a loss-making product then find a way to eliminate it from your activities.

Short-term cost reduction can be given a start by examination of the forty cost-reduction headings in Chapter 4, which should produce a number of ideas for early savings. The suggestions for revenue increase in Chapter 5 also include usable ways of turning a non-profitable activity into a profitable one.

Become liquid by balancing the books. Make sure that you keep the debtors' and creditors' levels relative to one another. Bring back in those outstanding debtor days and persuade your own creditors to allow you more time in line with the industry average (see Chapter 4). Put an embargo on all general overhead purchases and have all purchase invoices submitted to yourself or another director for approval. This will start to make an early reduction of inventories.

Together with other directors and senior managers, make the best assessment of likely workload for the next six months and use this to evaluate your requirements for labour and materials.

If calculations show that you have too much labour or materials then there is no merit in waiting to see if some unexpected upturn in trade occurs – it probably won't. Make arrangements to lower your labour cost by voluntary redundancies or early retirement, by part-time working, or even pay cuts. If you are at that time of the year when people expect annual wage increases, then announce that there will be no increases at this time – and make sure that it applies to everyone.

Insist on higher levels of performance. If you have measurement of individual, departmental, or factory levels of productivity then set higher targets and demand improvements quickly.

Think quantum improvement

You may be surprised at the amount of cost reduction or revenue increases which you will be able to achieve once you have determined this as your prime objective. Ask yourself what it would take not only to protect your profits but to increase them by 50 per cent:

- price increases of 5 per cent?
- material cost savings of 12 per cent?
- overhead reductions of 16 per cent?
- labour cost reductions of 30 per cent?
- or some combination of all these?

It may only mean realizing that something you are doing could be achieved in an entirely different way, and you could find yourself with a completely different cost structure. For example, when the engineering group TACE resited their head office with savings of some £2m, it increased their profits by 50 per cent! When Robert Horton took over as chairman of BP he cut out six layers of management. In the 1980s ICI reduced the head office headcount from 1200 to 400 people.

For historians and businessmen with long memories a glimpse of what can be achieved was afforded in Britain following the 1974 shorter working week. Although the country was forced into a three-day week, output fell by less than 5 per cent.

Yet the vision of industrial managers in the UK is still limited to measurement of improvement in productivity and profitability in lower single figure numbers. The 1988 CBI/PA survey concluded that most companies were happy to keep levels of productivity at current growth into the 1990s, but very few companies were seeking in excess of a 50 per cent surge in productivity. The report concluded, 'No quantum leaps are being sought.'

Four basic steps

Here are four important steps in profit-making. Within these steps lies the key to profitable operation and the avoidance of critical cashflow.

Step 1 Hold the barest minimum of material/component stocks and plan to receive supplies as dictated by the order book at the latest possible time before you need them.
Step 2 Plan the use of resources to reduce the job cycle time-scale to an absolute minimum.
Step 3 Arrange the earliest possible delivery of both the service or finished goods *and* the invoice.
Step 4 Achieve the quickest possible collection of payment for the goods.

Step 1 requires that the inventory of material and components is reduced to the lowest practical level. In most companies the achievement of minimum stock levels would by itself be sufficient to remove any pressure on the company's bank overdraft. This can only be achieved with good stock control systems and reliable sales department forecasts of customer requirements. The planned delivery of supplies to service the production line demands detailed production planning controls to align demand with capacity and material supplies.

Step 2 is the most ignored means of reducing costs. Only the very best production shops I have visited avoid the costly collection of work-in-progress 'mountains'. These piles of semifinished goods not only add to the production time-scale as they lie as inert as an oyster on the beach in August, but the cost of their idleness illustrates why actual profit never manages to equal the budgeted figure. Some companies have appointed short-cycle managers whose job is to shorten the time between receipt of order and the delivery of product and invoice, with some amazing results.

Step 3 requires the management of the production planning and control system to determine the anticipated completion date and to agree the earliest delivery date with the customer. Many manufacturing companies now plan to produce a customer's order only when the customer has specified a day and time for receipt into the customer's premises. I found a converse example of this at a client of ours who are factors of machinery, which they buy in from the manufacturer when a customer orders. What happens, however, is that customers delay the receipt of the machine into their premises until the last moment and thus delay payment of the deposit which is required before the machine is delivered. The total of the outstanding deposits in this company amounted to about 25 per cent of the total debtor list! In hard times, when customers take 70, 80, 90, or even more days to pay invoices, the important thing is to make sure that your invoice gets into the customer's sales ledger as early as possible. This should not be later than the day of despatch of goods. If your customers will accept invoices even before that date, so much the better.

Step 4, unless you are in one of those fortunate businesses which deal in cash, is the most important part of the whole process and must be done professionally. This means that you should engage competent credit controllers, or you should have the person responsible for your credit control trained up to professional standard. I have suggested in Chapter 4 methods which might assist in the collection of debts earlier, and any means which reduce debtor days to match cash-flow needs should be adopted.

There is no more important matter than the management of your cash flow. You may have to be aggressive with some customers, persuasive with others, charming with others, and persistent with the rest. It really does not matter how you do it, but you must match your incoming cheques with your

17

outgoing payments. Do not be frightened to use your solicitor, or to use the small claims court for amounts under £5000.

If you really want to bring your debtor days down from 90 to 65 you should perhaps consider using a factoring company. Firms using factoring companies, and there are now 10 000 in the UK, are paid on average 65 days after the issue of an invoice. Factoring allows companies to convert up to 80 per cent of sales invoices into cash within days by borrowing against them. There are two charges for using factoring companies: interest on the money advanced against the invoices, which is usually 3 per cent above bank base rate, and a service fee of up to 2.5 per cent of sales. Taking the average debt reduction from 90 days to 65 days, and assuming a service fee of 2 per cent, a company would reduce its debtor total by 28 per cent for just less than 5 per cent of the total debt. It is an alternative way of relieving the pressure on your overdraft facility at the bank.

Another way of reducing the amount owed, particularly by recalcitrant customers, is by encouraging them to pay part of their invoices. I know one credit controller who uses this method of prising money out of customers and has perfected it to a near art form. He calculates that the effect on the complete debtor list is to reduce the total by between 5 and 10 per cent.

The four-step plan suggested above aims to improve liquidity as follows:

- by reducing stock of materials and bought-in components;
- by reducing the time between purchase of materials and payment for them;
- by reducing the time the company is carrying the cost of materials, labour, and overheads by reducing the job cycle time;
- by early invoicing;
- by quicker collection of payments due.

The likely effect on liquidity in a typical company could be to improve it by a total equal to 50 per cent of net profit. This is a one-off improvement in cash flow, but it will also cut annual interest payments by up to 10 per cent of profit.

18

4

FORTY POTENTIAL AREAS OF COST REDUCTION

There are no profits inside a business, only costs.
                                            Peter Drucker

Having made the sale, management's job is to make the profit, and cost reduction is the principal route to the protection of those profits. This chapter examines the following six areas of cost and the potential for savings and profit enhancement:

Materials	Products
Money	Plant and machinery
People	Organization

Proper control of these areas could more than double company profits.

Nothing is cheap which is superfluous, for what one does not need is dear at a penny.
                                            Plutarch

Materials

The cost of materials is the highest of the major prime costs in manufacturing. In retailing and wholesaling, distribution, mining, transport, construction, plant hire, farming, local government, travel agencies, and the like, the cost of purchases of

19

non-labour items is as much as 70 per cent of all costs; the control of these costs is therefore not only important but essential to profitability.

You will find references in this chapter to the measurement of total stock value and the need to reduce it. Proper control is not possible, however, without measurement of materials and other purchases by category. Any advantage in achieving a constant or reducing amount of stock will be diluted if the inventory consists of a hard 'rump' of obsolete or slow-moving items. A control system that will give you accurate, up-to-date, comprehensive information should be installed, and you should then act on the information. I have been in companies where there was as much as two years' stock of certain items because no production control was in place. In tough times the need for liquidity is served well by having your assets in cash, not stock.

Stock control

In a year of no sales growth, good materials control could create savings equal to 50 per cent of net profit. You should consider stock as a drone; an idle, lazy, non-working drain on the company. Just by its existence it demands money, space, lighting, warmth, and attention; and contrary to what the balance sheet shows, stock is a liability not an asset.

Stock only what you must

If your control systems are good enough, why make or buy more than you can use? If your stock control system does not give you accurate, timely, and regular information on what you hold in stock and what you need to hold, then change your system.

This applies whether you are buying in materials or making components in house. I went into a company in the Midlands where there was no control over stocks of material and components at all. The machine-shop manager had a simple philosophy, which was to keep his machinists busy with whatever he thought needed making. We calculated over £100 000 worth of components in stock, so much, in fact, that they stopped buying and making components for four months. This was entirely the fault of production management, which did not keep any control information on stock or demand.

Stock only when you need to

When you buy goods too early:

- you pay for them earlier;
- you have to find room to store them;
- you have to have a system to tell you where they are;
- you run the risk of breakage, loss, or obsolescence.

JIT doesn't stand for Just Idle Theory – it works! Ask companies like Lucas, Hewlett-Packard, Rank Xerox, and Ford, all of whom have gone public on inventory reduction and related material savings through just-in-time practices.

Some stock-control systems use minimum stock levels to trigger off new orders when stock falls to a certain level. These trigger points should be adjusted regularly and downwards. The venture capitalist company, Schroder, even closed a warehouse at one company so that people had nowhere to hold stock.

If you order regular deliveries of materials, then buy more frequently: monthly instead of quarterly, or weekly instead of monthly. Be aware of your current stock needs as determined by the reality of the future order book, not the past orders trend.

Assume a company with £10m turnover, material costs of £4.5m, profits of £1m, and which turns its stock over six times per year. If the production planning and material controls are good enough to turn stock over eight times a year, it would achieve one-off savings of £219 000 and interest savings of £32 000 per annum (at 17 per cent interest). If stock were turned over ten times a year, savings would be £351 000 and £51 000 respectively, equivalent to 35 per cent profit increase in the first year and 5.1 per cent ongoing. But why stop at only ten times a year, why not twenty or thirty?

21

If you keep stock in several locations or depots, have you thought of centralizing it in order to reduce total stockholding? Satisfying customers by inter-branch transfers will have the same effect as reducing stocks. For more than a decade now, motor exhaust centres have operated centralized stock control. Each retail outlet holds only the stock to meet anticipated daily demand. The point-of-sale terminals are linked to the head office computer, and stock is replaced overnight.

Even small organizations can afford streamlined communications for improved stock control. I was involved in the selection of such a system for a glass and chinaware company with a central warehouse and three retail shops. This company implemented a centralized stock system which allowed it to reduce the stock at each shop, yet still responded to demand via computerized point-of-sale cash registers. The company saved £110 000 in stock reduction.

The great disappearing trick – shrinkage

If your fraud/theft/scrap/obsolescence is in double figures, take steps to reduce it. If you halved this source of stock losses, your profit margin could improve by 20 per cent.

The stories of under-priced motor spares which appear on the market are legion. Companies handling cash are particularly vulnerable. Every supermarket spends huge amounts of money taking precautions against 'shrinkage' by customers and staff. Audacious thieves even steal plant and vehicles – in fact, anything that moves and, on occasion, some things that don't. The introduction of computerized systems of control has provided another source of stock losses and dishonesty, bringing with it a new specialist, the computer security expert. You should get one to carry out a systems audit from time to time. If your stock control system is inefficient you can be losing money without knowing it. It doesn't have to be theft. Companies also receive invoices for goods they have not received or for different quantities than delivered.

I heard about an engineering sub-contract machine shop which had for years received and paid for brass and copper bars by weight. They did not realize, until traceability controls were introduced as part of BS5750 quality accreditation, that the company had been paying copper and brass rates for the weight of the wooden crates in which the bars were packed.

You should always check expense accounts; unauthorized purchases; unauthorized credit notes; overtime claims; book-keeping procedures; stock control procedures (particularly of high-value parts); stock discrepancies; invoices for goods you did not order; invoices for quantities you did not receive.

We shoot every third salesman

When visiting a potential new customer in Yorkshire, I was confronted in the reception area with a poster of a Wild West sheriff aiming a pistol. The caption read, 'We shoot every third salesman – and the second one's just left.'I wondered how the buyers or decision-makers exposed themselves to new products. The more established a company, the more vulnerable it is to a new competitor with new ideas and outlook.

I am told that 90 per cent of the materials and goods available to industry was not available ten years ago. The rate of change in materials and products in industry is dramatic, yet many of our buying habits are dictated by custom and practice. Making reductions in the cost of materials is an integral part of the annual budget and should be pursued daily by the person responsible for buying. You should review your purchasing policy by making time to examine new products/materials, by inviting different suppliers to tender, and by setting targets for reductions. All these should be monitored monthly. Remember, every 1 per cent saved on materials costs could increase your profit by 4 per cent.

Negotiate better discounts

The Scottish domestic appliance company, Norfrost, claims to buy the best materials and goods at the cheapest price, and they go to great trouble to negotiate the keenest prices:

- they place long-term orders but with frequent call-off – *for a discount!*
- they collect goods with their own transport – *for a discount!*
- they pay promptly – *for a discount!*

You do not necessarily have to pay early in order to get a discount. One of our clients pays at a specified date, *when they promised they would pay*, sometimes taking forty-five days – but the supplier allows a discount because payment is prompt and does not have to be chased. If, therefore, you are already paying promptly (and many companies do) you will be a good customer and you ought to push your creditworthiness for as much as you can. Do you have your terms and conditions on your purchase orders? Many companies do not, but these should tell your suppliers what you expect of them. They should state formally the standards of quality, service, and delivery which you require. It has been known for such an approach to produce offers of better discounts from suppliers who feel more confident dealing with professionals.

If you do not already see every purchase order, then arrange to do so for one month. Send back every purchase request with the instruction to the author to negotiate a better price – at least 5 per cent discount. Add up all the savings you have made in the month and then reset your purchasing budget to provide annualized savings at the same level – and expect your buyer to meet the new targets.

Always ask the price

Before placing a purchase order for goods, *always* ask for a quotation – even for a further supply of the same things, even from your oldest, most regular, most dependable supplier. Never simply order. Put the onus for price-setting on the supplier. In hard times the salesman may offer a discount if he thinks you are about to compare prices with another supplier.

In every company one will see frequent examples of staff reordering supplies of materials, stationery, printing, transport, computer supplies, and fuel, or booking air flights, train tickets, and hotel rooms without any questions about the cost.

In hard times this should be more controlled, either by firm instruction on the need for a price *before* ordering or by placing the negotiation for price with the professional buyer.

If staff are quoted a price increase when reordering supplies, the order should be withheld until confirmed by the buyer or director with purchasing responsibility.

Summary of potential savings

In manufacturing, wholesaling, and retailing the cost of materials is the highest single cost. Concentration on ways of keeping material usage and stocks to an absolute minimum can pay high rewards. Ways to reduce the cost of materials and components include:

- keener buying;
- better discounts;
- lower stock levels;
- less wastage and scrap;
- having suppliers hold materials either at their premises or yours;
- having customers supply materials free of charge;
- examining the purchase of cut-to-length material, or suppliers who will carry out secondary operations cheaper than you can.

The level of potential savings from better materials control can be very significant. For example:
Increase in number of times stock turned over = savings equal to 35 per cent net profit.
Better price negotiations (say 5 per cent) could equal 22 per cent profit increase.

Money

My problem is reconciling my gross habits with my net income.

Errol Flynn

The cost of money in businesses has been estimated to be at least 13 per cent of revenue by no less an authority than Peter Drucker, in his book *Managing for Results*. This includes working capital, interest charges, depreciation, and maintenance of plant and machinery. The probability is that this figure is lower than current UK money costs by several points.

A tip passed on by one of our fund-raising colleagues is that, if you buy in another country where lower interest rates apply, why not ask your suppliers to allow you longer credit, say 100 or even 120 days? In return, you offer to pay them the interest charged by their bank, which could be several points lower than in the UK.

The results of a cost-reduction questionnaire which we held at a recent profit-enhancement seminar makes interesting reading. It shows that, while people-related costs were identified as having most potential for improvement, better control of money was given a low priority in the improvement of profits.

Time is money

Figure 2 shows how the production and preproduction cycle can affect the cost of materials, labour, and overheads. This company buys in stock at month zero and pays for it two months' later (taking sixty days). The production cycle is two months, and the customer also takes sixty days to pay.

If the company has £1m turnover then annual costs of materials, labour, and overheads could equal £900 000 or £75 000 per month. The time-scale of Figure 2 shows the company carrying these costs for four months, equal to £300 000. If stock

Figure 2   Purchase time-scale

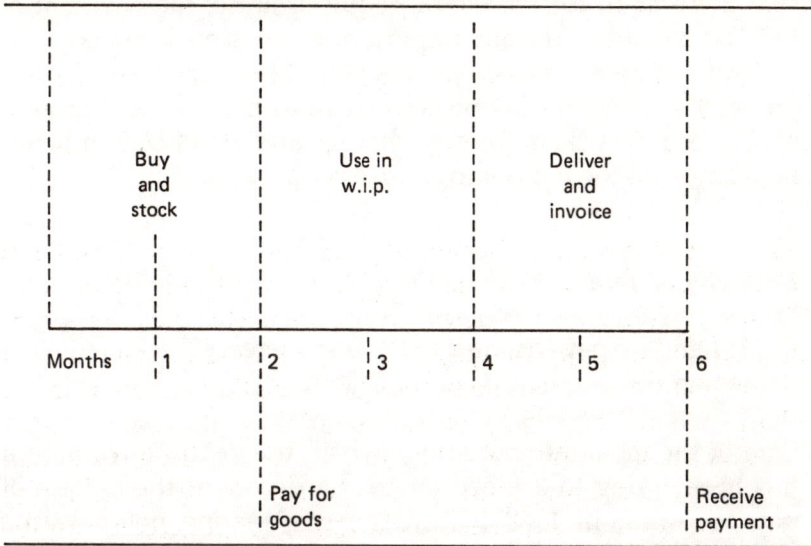

were ordered one month later this would increase liquidity by £33 750 (assuming material is 45 per cent of sales). If invoicing were one month earlier through reduced job cycle, that would release a further £75 000. Total benefits amount to £108 750 as a once-off reduction in borrowings, and £18 487 p.a. in interest.

Bill early

One way to reduce overdrafts is to send out invoices earlier. With customers taking eighty days and more to pay it is important to get your invoice in the queue as early as possible. The eighty days will not start until the customer has the invoice to hand, yet I know companies who still do not send out the invoice the same day as the goods. It's elementary, yet it doesn't happen. The cause might be that the computer will not allow this month's invoices to be entered until last month is closed off; or invoices cannot be sent out until a senior manager checks them; or on a time-and-material job all the costs are not to hand. Whatever the reason, change the system – now!

The value of outstanding invoices per day per £1 million turnover is typically £2700, and a reduction of five days in the period of debt collection could add more to profit than a 2 per cent increase in total sales. More importantly, the payment of £13 700 could be critically important to your bank manager.

Send out invoices by first-class post. For every £1m of sales, one day's reduction in outstanding sales invoices will mean a saving of £465 p.a. in interest charges and also £2739 in better liquidity – all for the cost of a first-class stamp.

Link pay to profit

Q   When is a pay increase not a cost increase?
A   When the tax man pays it for you.

One of the most difficult things which the British government has been trying to achieve for over a decade is the linking of pay to profit. In 1988 I heard an engineering union leader demanding the right to negotiate pay increases with profitable companies, free from any government pay guidelines or reference to the rate of inflation. The compelling attraction of that argument to employers is that first there must be a profit share.

In 1987 the government introduced a Profit Related Payment Scheme (PRP) under which up to half of an employee's bonus becomes free of income tax, provided it is calculated by a method linked to employer's profits and within a scheme registered with the Inland Revenue. In the 1991 Budget the profit-related pay was made free of all tax, up to prescribed limits. This means that if a PRP bonus was equal to 20 per cent of a person's pay, then at income tax levels of 25 per cent this is equal to a 5 per cent pay increase which the company does not pay. Employers negotiating a pay increase when staff expect 10 per cent and the company can only afford 5 per cent could satisfy the claim in full (and more) and yet still keep labour cost increases to 5 per cent by introducing a PRP scheme.

If you don't ask ... you don't get

You should think about asking your customers to pay for some of your costs, such as:

- storage costs for their packing materials;
- storage of your finished products held on call-off;

or to pay for goods or services

- with a deposit;
- staged payments;
- interest on overdue invoices.

It may depend on custom and practice in your industry but there are examples of companies in traditional manufacturing sectors, for example, who get money in advance, particularly from overseas customers.

Unlike other EC countries, a charge for interest on overdue accounts is not yet enforceable in law in the UK, although it could still be charged as part of a contract. EC harmonization rules may eventually change this in the UK, though I know a company in the equipment hire business which does charge interest now, and whenever a debtor has been taken to law the courts have allowed the interest charge.

A Gallup poll of 250 finance directors during the 1991 recession found that only 36 per cent of companies discount early payments or charge interest on late payments. Yet 93 per cent of those charging interest did not lose customers and were glad they introduced the system.

Keep what you earn

> *Money nowadays seems to be produced with a natural homing instinct for the Treasury.*
>
> Duke of Edinburgh

Are you paying the tax man too much? The business of paying the tax man only what he is legally entitled to is a very specialized subject. Ask any tax consultant about the likelihood of your company paying too much corporate tax, VAT, or national insurance, and he or she will be able to give you examples of tax-efficient ways of organizing your finances.

29

Timing is just as important to the finances of the company as it is to a comedian. Doing things at the right time is a very important principle when dealing with business taxation. A tax put off can be a tax saved. Here are five handy tips on timing.

(1) Defer a sale into the next accounting period.
(2) Bring a purchase forward into this period.
(3) Exchange a car after the year end.
(4) Capital allowance is best if you make a purchase on the last day of the year.
(5) Declare a dividend before the end of the year.

The company's cash flow will be improved if dividends are paid shortly before the end of the year, thus reducing the time between payment of advance corporation tax and its relief against mainstream corporation tax.

Do not delay payments to the point when you incur penalties. Make sure that the tax man cannot impose penalties for lateness or for error.

Keep accurate national insurance and PAYE calculations. If you get these wrong you can be liable not only for the employer's contribution of 10.45 per cent but also for any employee contribution which has not been paid.

There are also important VAT penalties for error and lateness. Customs and Excise are now able to apply a default surcharge for three late returns within any twelve-month period. It is also possible for a serious misdeclaration penalty of 30 per cent of the net VAT to be imposed. Not only are there penalties for lateness and error, but also interest on any outstanding amount at 12.5 per cent. This level of fines could obliterate the entire profits of a small company, so take this warning to heart.

The following are examples of tax-efficient financial control.

(1) A company was paying out short-lease premiums and not claiming any tax relief. It was advised to put in a claim for the past six years, and received a repayment of £12 000 plus tax-free interest of £4000.

(2) Another company voted a £300 000 bonus in the form of quoted shares. Done in the correct way this was treated as a

benefit in kind, not remuneration, and the company saved national insurance of 10.45 per cent (£31 350).

(3)   VAT and groups – if one company in a group exports, have it registered outside the group for VAT purposes. Provide monthly VAT accounts and secure repayment monthly.

(4)   Another group wound up a virtually dormant company in order to have fewer companies in the tax group – higher limits for small company rates, therefore lower tax bills.

(5)   A company had a large capital gain in the year. After looking at its investments in subsidiaries, two were found to be dormant and fully written-off. Negligible value claims were put in to crystallize a capital loss, which wiped out the liability on capital gains.

(6)   A shareholder wanted to withdraw from a business. Tax advisers structured a deal whereby the company bought back his shares in a particular way and the entire gain (proceeds £175 000) was covered by retirement relief. Other methods would have left him with a higher-rate tax liability.

(7)   A company had an office building constructed. Normally no allowances are available for this, but after analysis of costs, certain items were allowed as plant for tax purposes and saved tax of £28 000.

(8)   General planning advice for the year end can include the following: review of bonuses/dividend payments to decide which is cheaper; pay pension premiums before the year end to reduce profits; bring forward any contracts to purchase equipment, and therefore claim allowances in an earlier period.

It pays to get good professional advice. See your accountant before you take major financial decisions, but if your accountant is not a specialist tax adviser then find one who is.

Government assistance

There are still numerous ways of obtaining help from government sources. These include:

- Regional Selective Assistance (RSA): DTI
- Enterprise Initiative Schemes: DTI

31

- Training subsidies: TECs
- Regional Enterprise grants: DTI
- Export advice: DTI
- Research and technology assistance: DTI
- UK market data: Government Statistics Office
- New product development under SPUR and SMART: DTI

Despite the fact that Regional Selective Assistance is now a discretionary grant, there is a willingness by the DTI to support industry and commerce to develop new products and build new markets. If you are planning to spend money on site development, product development, exporting services, or improved communications, particularly if the project is innovative, my advice is to talk to the regional office of the DTI.

Guidelines for Regional Selective Assistance specify that the project must:

- be within an Assisted Area;
- be viable;
- contribute to the regional and national economy;
- create new, or safeguard existing, employment;
- be mainly funded by other sources of finance;
- not have started before approval.

As an example, a Midlands firm spent £500 000 (including additional working capital), created twenty-five jobs, and obtained £80 000 in Regional Selective Assistance.

Applications for assistance over £25 000 require a business plan, but the DTI will help with the cost.

Financial assistance is also available towards the use of consultants in the areas of design, marketing, production, quality control systems, and business planning.

Reduce the cost of company cars

If you want to cut 10 per cent from the bill for your company car fleet, ask ICI. One of their biggest divisions, Chemicals and Polymers, is extending the life of company cars before trade-in.

The working life of cars is being lengthened from three years or 40 000 miles to three and a half years or 70 000 miles.

Modern cars are capable of 70 000 miles or more with higher quality brought about by increased competition. As long ago as 1975 a UK consultancy company I worked for was retained by a large motor manufacturer to survey the main causes of corrosion in motor vehicles. Such research by all the car makers has paid off and now all major manufacturers are able to offer fleet users long-life vehicles. The manufacturers are victims of their own success, but that means that careful users can cut their costs.

Of course, the way to begin to control the cost of company cars, as with anything else, is firstly to know the costs. Make a sensible analysis by department and/or driver of running costs, tyre life, insurance claims, and trade-in value as a percentage of new value.

Unleaded petrol now has a lower fuel tax than the leaded variety, as well as being environmentally more friendly. Other ways to cut car costs include using diesel engines. You save money on the fuel and get more miles to the gallon. Soon, under European Community harmonization, diesel is likely to be around 25p per gallon cheaper than unleaded petrol. This cost benefit, together with 25 per cent better fuel economy than petrol engines, will soon make diesel engine running a very attractive option in reducing costs.

Prompt payment starts at the time of the sale

There seems to be little wisdom in researching the market, designing the right product, making it for the right price, and delivering it when the customer wants it, if you do not get paid for it.

Before the sale

Many bad debts can be traced to poor attention to detail at the time of the sale. Make sure that your salesmen do not get so carried away by the enthusiasm of the sale that they neglect the commercial considerations. Credit rating should start before the sale is approved. If the customer is a bad risk then all the chasing after unpaid invoices will be unproductive.

At the sale

Ask for payment in advance for new customers or slow payers. Terms and conditions must also be spelled out to the buyer. Your trade terms should be structured for the good of *your* cash flow, not that of your customers. If you let your customers extend their credit to three and four or even five and six months, you are playing banker for your customer – at zero interest.

If you produce quality products at the right price and delivered on time, you should be able to demand prompt payment. Be prepared to give discounts for early payment, but make sure the cost saving of the early payment is greater than the discount allowed.

After the sale

After delivery, do not hesitate to ask in increasingly strong terms for your money. Start debt-collection proceedings early rather than late. One company I know does its debt collection very well. After sending the invoice and the statement, the customer is telephoned two weeks before payment is due and asked if there is any problem about expecting payment on the due date. If there is a reluctance to confirm the date of payment, a problem-solving letter is forwarded to the customer asking for the name of the person responsible for payment and any reason for non-payment, such as the quality of service or goods supplied. If payment is not received and the services of a solicitor are used, the solicitor knows that there is no defence to the non-payment and a high court order can be sought.

The key to prompt payment of your invoice is to talk to your customers. Be frank. If you are confident of the quality of your service or product be equally confident about your right to be paid for it. Only by talking to your customers will you know if there is a problem. The aim of debt control is to reduce the time-scale of debt collection.

A rather robust way of prising money out of a reluctant debtor was suggested by one client. He suggested filling in a County Court form and sending a copy to the customer, accompanied only by a compliment slip. He maintains that it works better than a solicitor's letter.

Some companies leave the debt-collecting to untrained people, but this is a fatal error. At one of our client's, a recent end-of-month analysis of the debtors revealed a total of £721 000. When the category of debtors was completed, it was found that the credit controller could only chase up £150 000 of the debt; the rest of the total included disputed debts, customers requiring credit notes, some written-off totals, and some new debts. It will be appreciated, therefore, that analysis of the debtors list is an essential prerequisite to engaging someone to chase debts and reduce the debtor total.

In a survey carried out by the CBI covering four hundred small and medium-sized companies at the end of 1990, it was stated that the growing problems of cash flow pressure could make the difference between success or failure for a number of firms. Member companies of the CBI were urged to pay bills on time after the survey showed that almost one in five small businesses was in danger of going under because of delayed payment. Almost 70 per cent of the companies said that delays ranged up to forty-five days beyond the agreed payment date, while 20 per cent said they had to wait more than thirty days longer than that.

It was estimated that the cost of allowing an extra month's credit to a business with a turnover of £2m a year was running at £29 000 per annum. It is the lack of money in the business, however, which often delivers the killer blow. The earlier deposit of bills collected one month sooner is more important than the cost of servicing the overdraft.

Turnover isn't everything

Two Polish farm lads had heard of free-market enterprise and decided to go into business themselves. They bought a lorry and filled it with cabbages which they bought at 20 zloties each. They took them into town on market day and sold them all – at

20 zloties each! At the end of the day, therefore, they had exactly the same amount of money as they had at the start. One of the lads turned to the other and said, 'There, you see, I told you we should have got a bigger lorry!'

Increases in turnover do not necessarily lead to increased profit. In fact, it is quite possible for the reverse to occur. I recently visited a fast-growing engineering subcontractor which was a model of enterprise and hard work. They are fearful of raising prices and some customers have refused to accept increases for the past two years, even though costs have gone up. In order to maintain levels of profit the company is 'buying-in' extra work at unprofitable prices in the mistaken belief that this will support the company growth. They have chronic cash-flow problems.

On the other hand, I know a builders' merchant who decided to stop supplying to bad payers. The result was that he certainly had a lower turnover but the ending of extended credit gave him just as much profit – and an easier life.

The managing director of one of my clients gave me this piece of advice which should be posted up in all growing companies:

Turnover is vanity; profit is sanity.

Knowledge is the key: know which products are profitable, know which customers are profitable, know which market is profitable, then work at increasing the profitable ones.

People

We lost because we told ourselves we lost.
Leo Tolstoy, *War and Peace*

People costs may not be the biggest single cost centre, but the people factor has the most important influence on company profitability. For people to operate well in an effective way they must be capable, trained, motivated, rewarded, and controlled.

Whether it is the leadership style of the chief executive or the ability of middle management or the attitude of the employees or the presentation of the sales team, people make your company what it is.

Switching people on

Have you ever wondered why a clock-watching storekeeper will spend weekends digging a swimming pool for spastic children? Or your senior typist gives up her holiday to work twenty-four hours a day running a Guide camp? Or your supervisor spends twenty hours a week training to run a marathon? There are other questions, related to your business, which you might ask yourself. How do you get your employees to be better than your competitors? How do you improve the company performance? How can two of your people be as effective as three of the competition? The answer is *motivation*, and there are many things which affect the motivation of the individual: working conditions, style of management, responsibility, and interesting work, as well as pay and rewards.

At the time of writing it is predicted that the UK annual rate of inflation is set to reduce to less than 5 per cent, although wages and salaries are set to rise by 7 per cent. Employees will expect to be able to negotiate wage increases of 7 per cent because of the expectation of improvement in their standard of living and the disbelief in the promised low inflation rate. All that makes it difficult to negotiate low pay increases and, even if you succeed, low wages will not attract good people. It is very satisfactory to attract high performers through good pay and conditions; it is better still to be paying higher wages out of increased profits.

Control labour cost drift

In hundreds of companies visited, I cannot remember a single one where people productivity could not be increased by 10 per cent or, put another way, where unit labour cost could not be cut by 10 per cent.

Calculate 10 per cent of your company wage bill, and add it to your net profit. It will probably increase it by 15 to 20 per cent (British Aerospace would add 60 per cent to profits for a 10 per cent cut in the wage bill, as was mentioned in Chapter 1). Better still, imagine cutting labour costs by 25 per cent, as some of our clients have done. This will in all likelihood add 40–50 per cent to your pre-tax profits.

Trying to control labour costs is like trying to close the lid of your suitcase at the end of a holiday – if you squeeze it at one end it pops up at the other. If your labour rates are low there will be pressure on bonus payments; if you control bonus payments there will mysteriously appear a need to work overtime.

The only way to know whether your wage bill is rising or falling is by calculating overall figures. Regardless of the individual product costings, be sure about the ratio of total wages to total production. My tip for controlling unit labour cost is to measure overall labour cost as a percentage of total sales:

$$\frac{\text{Total wage bill}}{\text{Total sales or units produced}} \times 100$$

No labour cost will escape such a calculation. Calculate this figure monthly and plot the trend. Make sure it does not rise. If it does, take action. Cut out all overtime. Make your managers control their staff to produce the goods in normal time.

In 1980 when the US car industry was going through a recession, one of the major manufacturers encouraged technical and support staff to leave undone the bottom 20 per cent of jobs on their priority list. The result was that all overtime was stopped yet all important work was done.

Many company managers are prevented from reducing labour costs, partly because they do not know what the true costs are, and partly because they have no means of controlling them. The lack of accurate labour standards, of levels of performance, utilization, and effectiveness, prevents cost-reduction exercises from even starting; if you do not measure, you cannot control. My experience tells me that you will improve the effective use of a resource (people, plant, or money) by 5 per cent just by paying attention to it.

Even a simple exercise like examining timesheets and producing regular, if only rudimentary, reports on time attended, work produced, and time on and off productive work, could be sufficient to save 5 per cent or even more!

Overheard in the Canteen

'I like this job but my last place paid more money, with shorter hours and longer holidays.'

'Why did you leave then?'

'Oh, they went broke!'

How many people do you need?

If you believe the suggestion in the previous section that there is at least 10 per cent more people productivity capacity than you use, then how can you match staffing levels with labour requirements in an efficient way?

In a recession many managers attempt to keep their workforce busy producing stock, even if demand has fallen. Foremen and department supervisors have been conditioned by the creed of maximizing labour utilization. It will be difficult for them to appreciate the wider priority of the conservation of cash unless it is fully explained to them.

How do you determine your manning levels? You do not need constant high manning levels to meet the occasional peak demand. Furthermore, this is not just a blue-collar-worker exercise; now that office workers are nearly as numerous as blue-collar employees, their performance and cost are just as critical as what we call 'direct labour'. This means that quality can apply to office work as well as the shop floor. Giving office staff the right tools, environment, and atmosphere could pay off in increased effectiveness. Computerization now enables electronic mail for the generation and delivery of internal memos.

How many hours of labour time do you pay for which is not available for productive work because of absenteeism, lateness, long lunch hours and tea breaks? As Dale Carnegie said, 'The list of time-wasting activities is endless.'

All activities – shop floor, office, and management – require appropriate performance measures so that a programme of continuous improvement can be introduced and the right number of people employed.

There's always a better way

For more than seventy years now the structured study of the methods used in production (and even in office work) has been practised in work study, with universally successful results in reducing complexity in manufacturing operations. There is therefore nothing new in the method-improvement route to cost reduction.

Work-study and method-study technicians examining the what, when, where, how, who, and why of each operation can produce amazing results. One of our clients recently reduced the cost of manual operations in a plant making exhaust systems by over 20 per cent. Another company changed the manning on a conveyorized oven to increase labour productivity by 5 per cent and plant utilization by 15 per cent, purely as the result of a half-day method-study exercise.

You should expect your production engineers to reduce product costs by 10 per cent per annum. If you do not have full-time engineers then set a more modest 5 per cent cost-reduction target and encourage managers, foremen, and direct operatives to achieve it. In our typical manufacturing company with 60 per cent costs absorbed in labour and material requirements, a 10 per cent cost reduction will add 60 per cent to pre-tax profits.

> *Method is like packing things in a box; a good packer will get in half as much again as a bad one.*
>
> Lord David Cecil

Are wages and salaries reducible?

I know many companies where management treat wages and salaries as fixed costs. The idea that people must have more this year than last is one of those rules which may have to be suspended in tough times. It is not unknown for companies to suspend pay increases in times of recession: at the beginning of 1991, two very large companies, Phillips and Michelin, imposed a pay freeze for nearly 30 000 workers in the UK.

Struggling in the recession, Phillips, with its electronic products ranging from computers to car radios, lost 60 000 employees worldwide in 1991. The postponement of a pay increase of, let us say, 8 per cent for six months gave Phillips UK £7m better liquidity. Other companies adopting a wage freeze in the recession included London Carriers International, British Steel, British Airways, *The Guardian*, the *Manchester Evening News*, and Barclays Bank. National Westminster Bank's investment banking subsidiary, County Natwest, even introduced pay cuts averaging 20 per cent in that period, and Thomas Cook, the UK's second-largest travel agent, asked staff to take pay cuts of up to 10 per cent.

This subject of pay is one factor which separates the serious survivor from the rest. Company managers do not deal with people problems very well. The reasons are humane and laudable, and when the problem is irresistible the usual 'knee-jerk' reaction is to make people redundant. There are, however, at least six other steps which can be taken and which might be more cost effective.

(1) Freeze pay increases, as Phillips and Michelin did.
(2) Cut out all overtime.
(3) Cut out all bonuses.
(4) Reduce benefits.
(5) Work part time.
(6) Reduce pay.

The above will only be effective for a limited period; when things get better reward loyalty by restoring and increasing salaries.

41

Reducing the wages and salary bill without making people redundant has the merit of sending out a positive message – 'Everyone is important, we shall survive, times will get better, we want this team to stay.'

Ask more from your key people

In every organization there is a handful of key decision-makers. In the larger companies this could amount to twenty people; in smaller firms it might be no more than six. These people are probably already giving you 100 per cent effort. In a period of recession, why not explain the company trading and financial situation and ask them to give you 10 per cent more hours? If they are properly motivated (and they should be, if they are your important decision-makers) they will do it just to help the company.

This 10 per cent more hours should be used not in doing more of managing the same things in the same way, but in cost-reducing exercises in some specific area such as value analysis, plant utilization improvement, reduction in absenteeism, quality improvement, debtor days reduction, negotiating better discounts, and so on.

If the 10 per cent more effort results in improved or contained profits you will need to reward this additional workload. Pay is not the only way to reward key people, and you can even reduce company costs when paying bonus or profit shares in other than cash. Benefits which are considered valuable include pension schemes, share option schemes, company cars, medical insurance, and service awards. Some of these non-cash benefits are tax efficient, as money paid as salary costs the company an additional 10.45 per cent in National Insurance, although the Inland Revenue are taking increasing interest in 'benefits in kind' and finding new ways to value them for tax purposes.

Provide incentive and reward

One of my favourite stories is about the successful business tycoon who takes his graduate recruits up to the top of a hill overlooking a lush valley with executive houses with swimming pools, two-car garages, and so forth. He says to them, 'If you work very hard, long hours, no holidays, without pay increases, then one day all this will belong to me!' Your employees will help you to be more profitable if you share the vision of your company as a growing business venture in which they have a stake in its success.

I know of a company who had a severe results-orientated incentive scheme for its sales force, which consisted of a low basic pay but high on-target earnings. They recruited a highly motivated salesman who met his targets so well that his earnings were higher than the managing director's, so they altered the scheme to reduce the potential earnings. The salesman left.

Another company asked us to design a sales department incentive scheme which paid a high bonus based on sales contribution. Last year the most successful salesmen doubled their pay and the company are delighted. Norfrost, the Scottish freezer manufacturer, pays a penny to each employee for every freezer which gets through its quality checks, which adds £30 to weekly pay.

In 1988 I was called in by a company in the trim and graphics business whose incentive scheme was not producing savings. Upon examination it was not surprising that the scheme did not provide sufficient incentive. The payment slope was so shallow that increases in output of 28 per cent only paid 14 per cent more money.

The best schemes are those which pay wage increases relative to production increases: for example, 25 per cent bonus for 25 per cent more output. Manufacturing companies should not fear such sharp bonus payments, as for every 1 per cent increase in labour costs the company will save at least 2 per cent in overhead recovery.

There is a warning about potentially high bonus schemes, however. Make sure that the targets are set using meaningful units of measurement. For example, salesmen who have discretion about selling prices should not be measured on sales value but on contribution; executives should be measured on profits or return on investment or similar overall indicator; heads of department should be measured on unit labour costs or plant utilization or departmental efficiency or other multifactor calculation.

There is nothing wrong in paying good bonuses or sharing profits if the bonuses are earned by reduced costs or increased profits.

Know what you want to achieve

Identifying the purpose of an incentive scheme is an important prerequisite.

- Do you want to reduce unit labour costs?
- Do you need to increase output?
- Do you need to increase pay?
- Do you want to reward increased profitability?
- Do you want to retain key people?
- Are you unable to keep delivery promises?

In only one of the above questions is the answer necessarily to introduce an incentive scheme – all but the first need can be met without increased productivity.

- Output can be increased by employing more people or working overtime.
- Pay can be increased if you can get the customers to fund the increase.
- Reward for past profitability can be tax efficiently achieved by introducing a profit-related pay scheme.
- The pay of key people can be accommodated within a properly structured pay and salary structure or using job analysis or merit rating.
- Improvement in delivery dates will be better achieved via production control and associated techniques.

Even if you have identified improvements in costs or profits as the prime objective, it is possible to achieve that without an incentive scheme through methods, motivation, and measurement, although it is likely that incentives would help.

Senior management must be committed to the scheme

Once you have decided that an incentive scheme is right for you, the detailed communication, administration, and implementation must be carried through with conviction and enthusiasm by senior management, whose supportive action must be visible.

> *Three out of four UK companies do not benefit significantly from their productivity-related payment scheme.*
> CBI/PA Productivity Survey, 1988

People are better than you think

Robert Townsend, in his book *Up The Organization*, tells the story of when he took over Avis Car Rental. He was told by the outgoing president that all his staff were useless and needed replacing. Three years later the same people had been promoted and three identified as potential chief executives!

Another example is the change at the engineering group TI. Since Chris Lewinton arrived as chief executive in 1986, he has completely rationalized the group of companies, with fifty main subsidiaries reduced to eleven over four years. The development of core businesses in mechanical seals, tube-making, specialized engineering, and thermal technology has made TI an international player and reduced its exposure to the UK economic cycles. Operating profits rose from 5.5 per cent in 1986 to 12.2 per cent in 1990, and product development is towards more sophisticated, higher value-added products. In the 1980 recession, although the company cut half its 60 000 workforce, only a handful of its subsidiaries was profitable. Perhaps the most important development at TI is the way

45

management has changed. The new mood of determination has been achieved by a management team most of whom were already with the company when Lewinton arrived.

People will give you increased profits if you tell them what you expect. I know many company directors and managers who keep budget figures and expected target times to themselves, even though such standards will have been used to determine selling prices and, therefore, must be achieved or bettered to make a profit. People want to do a better job and to be developed as far as they can, both individually and as a team.

If your priority is to become more profitable, then tell them. If they need to learn new people-management skills, budgetary control techniques, or computer systems, then train them. Your people will get as much satisfaction from doing a bigger job as from getting more pay. They will reduce costs if you set that as a priority and give people the means and support to achieve it.

Tom Farmer of Kwik-Fit says, 'We operate personnel programmes which are based on respect for the individual and which cater for his or her financial aspirations and career development. In addition to the pay package, working people need motivation.' This is a company which in the four years to 1987 had increased turnover by 136 per cent but profits by 314 per cent.

The Japanese Government is actually considering introducing a law to force people to take all their paid holidays – only half of the labour force take all their due holidays. Peer pressure rather than love of the job means that the average Japanese worker puts in 200 hours a year more than Americans and Britons and 500 hours more than French and West Germans.

DIY cost reduction

In a recession there is an urgent need to improve efficiency, and the ideas of your staff are a very important source of profit protection through the elimination of unnecessary costs.

Ironically, creative talent seems to thrive in difficult times. Whether this is because of the survival instinct or because managers are more open to ideas or because of improved teamwork is not clear, but use this opportunity to harvest the wealth of money-saving ideas which exists in every company but which so often remains untapped. Companies don't spend money, people do, and the people who know most about how to reduce your spending are the people who do the spending – your employees. Get your staff to reduce costs by asking them to set their own cost-reduction budgets.

You will probably have to pay to encourage ideas, but as the awards will be based on proven savings there will not be any doubt about the justification for paying. Successful schemes pay out between 10 per cent and 20 per cent of first-year savings. You may not need to set up a formal suggestion scheme. Encourage departments to set their own savings targets. They will own them and achieve them.

Other companies have achieved great success in the implementation of such schemes – BT saved £1.5m in the four years to 1988, Austin Rover saved £1.5m in 1986, and Lucas factories saved £1m in 1987, all from internal suggestions from their employees.

Employ and keep good people

To be able to manage your company properly, you have to have the right people in key jobs. To get the right people you will have to pay the going rate for good people. This is one of those paradoxes: increase your costs in order to make savings.

Aim for a high sales-per-employee ratio. Five years after they started, Apple Computers had the best ratio in the business – the semiconductor industry had a ratio of sales per employee of $35 000 p.a., IBM had $155 000, and Apple had $250 000. Founder Steve Job puts it down to employing exceptional people.

It has already been said that people are important, and there is just as much maintenance needed to keep people operating efficiently as with plant and machinery. The cost of replacing a person in my company is estimated at about £5000. This is direct costs excluding training and the effect of a learning curve on job efficiency.

If you lose a person through bad human resource management or poor communications or conditions, you can write off as much as 5 per cent of your profit! If you keep ten people from leaving by good human relations practices or management attitude/culture (call it what you like) you probably affect the profit levels of your company better than if you sold an extra £300 000 worth of goods. Or put it another way: if you run a company with, say, twenty people and you keep four people from leaving through good employee practices/culture/ attitude, you will probably affect profit levels better than an increase in turnover of 20 per cent.

Products

> *Employers don't pay wages – they only handle the money.*
> *Products pay wages.*
>
> Henry Ford

The previous pages contain ideas about cutting existing cost levels, but that is to assume that the present cost is what it should be. It is often worth spending time and money to determine the right cost of products and services.

The cost of an industrial or production engineer to arrive at the optimum labour and material cost in a product should provide the means of identifying prime cost savings worth at least five times the engineer's salary.

A great way to reduce costs is to change your product or service to take out some of the costs, so drive down the standard cost of products by systematic examination of every cost source.

Remember that a 5 per cent reduction in prime costs in a typical company will increase profits by at least 30 per cent.

How much should it cost?

The main cost of a product is in the prime or direct use of labour and materials. These, we know, are likely to be 60–70 per cent in most companies.

Product costs can change over a period of time because different materials and equipment have become available, or associated parts and fittings may have been changed, or else the customer may no longer require all the features of the product, or perhaps it was made in a particular way in order to meet an emergency and has not subsequently been corrected. Company cost systems often fail to reflect these changes.

It is important to determine the lowest material and labour cost consistent with the quality of the product required. This 'standard' becomes the target for all management activity. If it is set higher than it needs to be the achievement of the correct cost level will never become a management priority.

In the early 1980s I was asked to lead a value analysis team in the examination of ways to reduce the costs of producing filing cabinets. The most popular filing cabinet is the four-drawer model, which outsells all others and there is thus much competition for the business. The team was given the task of reducing the cost of the cabinet from £36 to £29, at which level huge contracts were available. The investigation examined different designs, materials, methods of assembly, painting, and packaging. We actually reduced the cost to just below £28 by a methodical approach and good teamwork.

The profitability of a product does not depend only on the direct costs of material and labour but also on the cost of management and technical and support staff. To allocate a fixed average overheads cost to a new product that is absorbing much marketing, design, research, prototype, production, or packaging costs is plainly understating the case. At the end of a mature product life cycle, on the other hand, average overheads allocation may be too much.

Accurate and detailed knowledge of true product costs is another of these areas of control which is vital to successful company management. If your prices for simple products are high because of wrong cost collection, the competition will drive you out of the market-place; if your prices for complex products are underpriced, the competition will let you have all the business you can handle, as very soon you will no longer be a competitor.

Total quality approach to everything

The attitude of making things 'right first time' is a key source of profit enhancement. Placing the responsibility for quality which is built-in (not added on) with the producer of the product or service reduces the involvement, and the cost, of other non-essential personnel.

Motivation, pride, right attitude, good communication, and customer satisfaction are valuable quality improvement requisites, but the difficulty is in trying to prove it. Companies without accurate prime product and overhead costs are not likely to generate figures on rework, scrap, lateness, credit repayments, increasing transport costs, management time, quality control department costs, and the like. Every work-bench and desk should therefore have pinned over it the following paraphrase of a quote by Kwik-Fit's Tom Farmer: 'We make things that don't come back for customers who do.'

The 'right first time' target is not a new 'holy grail'. In 1966 I worked as a productivity officer for the British Productivity Council. Among over 250 companies in Lancashire there was an awareness that there was a better way towards a higher quality level. Over the years since 1966 there have been attempts to raise national awareness of the need for improved quality such as Quality and Reliability Year 1966, National Strategy for Quality 1978, and now the almost universal requirement for companies to have quality levels to BS5750. Now that the Japanese have shown us that quality management *is* possible and effective, we must learn to compete in domestic and world markets before others with better and cheaper goods consign British industry to a place in history.

The Edwards Deming seven-part action plan for business transformation contains this practical gem: 'Divide every company activity into stages, identify the customer of each stage as the next stage. Continual improvement of methods should take place at each stage, and stages should work together towards quality.'

This concept of the next user in the organization being the customer does not only apply to production operations. I experienced a salutary lesson in this when I was a design draughtsman some years ago, and we were developing a plant for the production of a new product. I was, almost literally, dragged out of my office one day by the plant maintenance manager who led me precariously up a ladder to the top of the structure I had designed and pointed out the complete inaccessability of an adjustment screw for one of the pulleys. The fitter could hardly reach it and the bolt-head could not be turned with a spanner in a confined space – unless the fitter was a contortionist!

Value analysis

Value analysis is a systematic and analytical technique used to examine all the functions and costs of an existing item, product, system, or activity, in order to determine if any cost item can be reduced while maintaining or improving the functional requirements.

This approach to cost reduction is probably more effective than any other. Its purpose is to reduce the cost of any product, process item, or activity while at the same time maintaining or improving the function. The beauty of this very practical technique is that the results are measured by the amount of money saved – for example, the food giant H.J. Heinz saved £2m a year by eliminating the label on the back of ketchup bottles.

In most organizations method-study and work-study exercises are directed towards the reduction of labour costs. A more profitable approach, because it includes wider costs, can be achieved by value analysis of major items of materials and overheads. In many instances the investigation will reveal the possibility of eliminating a part altogether, and there is no more complete or purer cost-reduction exercise than one which reduces the cost to zero.

51

Individuals in the course of their day-to-day work seldom use their full creative ability. Apparent lack of time encourages the acceptance of previously used methods, designs, processes, and procedures. Even when original work is being developed, the 'first idea that works' is often adopted. Value analysis, however, lists all the ideas but develops only those which will be lowest in cost for the function to be performed.

One of the most impressive examples of the use of value analysis is to be seen at a domestic appliance factory in Warrington. There two full-time value engineers have made prime cost savings of just over 1.5 per cent of turnover in two and a half years. As the programme is ongoing this will represent seven-figure annual reductions in direct costs as new investigations reveal savings on new products. The senior value engineer says, 'Ten per cent cost reduction is a reasonable target. Keep the numbers of projects down to those you can implement quickly. There is a trade-off between utilizing VA engineers' time on lots of projects and concluding projects quickly.'

Some examples of recent cost cutting activities include the following.

Example 1 Grill-pan brander grid changed to enamel, with the advantages of cleaning convenience and a better marketing feature, resulting in savings of £45 000 p.a. materials and labour.

Example 2 Mixing-tube material specification investigation resulted in a new specification, saving 32 per cent of materials cost.

Example 3 Manifolds now made by die-casting instead of using bar material, with the benefits of JIT delivery and better 'O'-ring fitting, resulting in savings of 37 per cent in the purchase price after a ten-month pay-back.

Example 4 Redesign of support door plunger and catch assembly, with the benefit of standardization of widths and resultant savings of 15 per cent in door assembly costs.

Another value engineer explained that other ideas for cost reduction come also from other employees and listening to suppliers. The changeover from hot foil badge-making to in-house thermal transfer labelling, for example, has saved 39 per cent of costs, and this idea came from discussions with makers of thermal transfer equipment. The company suggestion scheme has also produced ideas such as the one to reduce the need for self-tapping holes and assembly operations for three separate parts by redesign to eliminate the screws and replace by spot-welding. The VA team now have some thirty current projects with probable or possible savings estimated at another £1m. There is always a better way!

The employment of a dedicated cost-reduction engineer with likely savings in the ratio of ten times salary costs, even in times of recession (or particularly so), could lead to £200 000–£300 000 annual savings. For companies with at least £5m turnover, a full-time VA engineer must be a near-certain route to improving profits by anything up to 40 per cent. For smaller companies it will be difficult to justify a full-time VA engineer, in which case the use of a VA consultant to lead an internal team, part time, might be appropriate.

Plant and machinery

> *Work smarter, not harder or longer.*
>
> F.W. Taylor

Fill in the peaks and troughs

The effectiveness of plant is determined by the efficiency at which it operates when running, and for how long it can be run. Utilizing all your assets to the optimum is a simple way of reducing costs. It applies to plant and machinery, vehicles, premises, space, and people. If you can manage these resources so that they produce longer or with fewer interruptions or more efficiently, it will have a marked effect on profits.

You carry the cost of depreciation of plant, machinery, and vehicles whether they produce or not. You have paid the capital cost and implementation cost and the cost of space used by machines whether they are idle or working. If you can keep them working or, with better planning, tooling, and maintenance, get them working more productively, then the goods produced will be at a lower unit cost.

Improved utilization includes working longer hours; shift or 24-hour working; better maintenance; filling in troughs with other work; improved set-up times; reduced down-time; standardizing products; better planning; more efficient materials control; better decision making, and subcontracting your spare capacity. The company that keeps its employees and machinery working for more than 75 per cent of the working day is the exception, yet if you get twenty minutes a day extra output out of your people or plant, you could well add over 20 per cent to your profits.

Investment – not speculation

This is a plea for controlled investment. You lose all or much of the labour cost by automated plant, so the rewards from sound investment in modern machinery can be dramatic. Even the proper maintenance or updating of existing plant can bring lower costs and improved profits through higher operating speeds or lower running costs. Remember that there is always a better way, which might in certain circumstances be to automate a manual operation.

However, a period of recession may not be the time to risk capital reserves on hopeful changes. Investment with near-certain returns from properly investigated and costed labour or material savings is not to be confused with spending which has no measured or predetermined benefits.

In the middle of the 1991 recession the Huddersfield-based Holliday Chemical Holdings spent £160 000 on computerized materials requirement planning. The system is expected to reduce the £8m stock level by £1m. That is what I call return on investment.

If you are tempted to spend as a 'knee-jerk' reaction to profit problems remember that the best decision-makers only get half their decisions right and any expenditure that is ill thought through probably has less than a 50 per cent chance of success.

Remember Mark Twain's advice: 'There are two times when one should not speculate – when you can't afford it, and when you can!'

A cost centre shared is a cost centre halved

It may be possible to share the cost of some of your activities with other companies, such as transport, computer services or equipment, office services, buying, training, or advertising.

It might be cheaper to set up a shared transport company or centralized computer than use a haulage contractor or a bureau. Another option might be to engage people part time in these activities.

It could certainly be more cost beneficial to engage specialist personnel part time or as required, and activities which lend themselves to part-time or occasional manning include book-keeping, technical specialisms, personnel regulations, recruitment, safety, training, computer operating, and computer programming.

Business in the Community, the umbrella organization of Britain's enterprise agencies, helps small companies to combine limited budgets and management resources to break into new markets. Co-operative marketing agreements are common in many continental countries, and 10 per cent of all Italian exports, for example, are done via such a group.

The Consort Hotels organization has 250 UK hotels that make up to 20 per cent savings on centralized purchasing; there is a centralized booking system, and the group provides brochures for its mainly single hotel members.

Think bottlenecks

The simple clue to improving plant efficiency

Balancing the different parts of production is a very complex thing. It is unlikely that your raw material stores, machine shop, paint shop, assembly, packaging, warehousing, and despatch are all working at the same high level of performance or productivity or throughput. It is likely that one of these areas of production is working flat out, even working overtime, while others will have spare capacity. The problem of optimum utilization can be addressed in two ways, depending upon whether additional output can be sold or not.

Table 2   Normal labour utilization

	Output per day	Utilization %	No. employed	Labour utilized	People required
Preproduction	1000	90	5	0.5	4.5
Machine shop	1000	85	20	3.0	17.0
Paint shop	1000	105	8	(0.4)	8.4
Assembly	1000	95	25	1.25	23.75
Packaging	1000	80	10	2.00	8.00
Despatch	1000	75	5	1.25	3.75
		Totals	73	7.6	65.4

Labour utilization $\dfrac{65.4}{73}$ =   89.6%

Table 3   Labour utilization as a result of increased demand

	Output per day	Utilization %	No. employed	Labour utilized	People required
Preproduction	1100	99.0	5	0.05	4.95
Machine shop	1100	93.5	20	1.3	18.7
Paint shop	1100	115.5	8	(1.24)	9.24
Assembly	1100	104.5	25	(1.13)	26.13
Packaging	1100	58.0	10	1.2	8.8
Despatch	1100	82.5	5	0.87	4.13
		Totals	73	1.005	71.95

Labour utilization : 98.56%

Table 2 illustrates labour utilization for a notional output of 1000 units per day, while Table 3 shows the effect of increased demand. If sales demand can sustain an increased output of 10 per cent to, say, 1100 units per day, then the paint shop output should be increased either by working additional hours or by increased performance. An easing of the paint shop bottleneck has produced 10 per cent more production through the plant with 10 per cent increase in overall labour utilization for only 2.7 per cent increased labour cost. On the other hand, if you cannot sell the additional capacity then you have too many people or too much plant or too much space – get rid of the surplus.

Bottlenecks do not only apply to manufacturers. If you are in wholesaling, retailing, transport, advertising, contracting, or whatever, you will have departments which rely on each other and need to be balanced for maximum efficiency.

The cost of space

In 1980 a company in the West Midlands built a 200 000 sq. ft. factory, which included 25 000 sq. ft. of warehouse to store aluminium ladders and domestic hardware. The company policy was to make for stock and to have six weeks' supply always available, so the warehouse was designed to hold about 100 000 items. The cost of the warehouse, with six-high racking, special high-sided pallets and reach trucks, was about £500 000.

A visitor to the factory today will find a near-empty warehouse and a just-in-time production-control policy in which assembly schedules are only finalized after the customer has gone firm on a delivery date into his own store. The investment in the now empty warehouse has been made obsolete by better communication between supplier and customer, one aspect of a just-in-time approach to manufacturing.

Is there potential for reducing the cost of working space in your company? Areas worthy of investigation include:

- current use of space: has need changed?
                          do you need it all?

- current cost of space;
- current location: do you need to be in the city centre with rent at a premium and with the extra cost of parking and travelling?
- premises: can you share? or sub-let? (The main profit source of some companies is sub-let premises.)
- can people work from home and save office space?

A circular from the Treasury sent to all government departments recommends allowing tax inspectors, and other civil servants who spend much of their time out of the office, to work from home to save office accommodation costs and travel expenses. The main purpose of the move, it is claimed, is to gain access to a wider pool of labour and to retain skilled and experienced staff.

We have a client who rents off a corner of his works to a car repairer, a net £20 000 p.a. straight on to the bottom line (last year that was equal to 30 per cent of net profit).

Marks & Spencer gets almost twice the sales per unit of shelf space as its competitors. So ask yourself, do you need all the space you have? Just think how unused space drains your profit level through the cost of rates, heating, lighting, and maintenance.

Organization

> Run, then, in such a way as to win the prize.
> St Paul's First Letter to the Corinthians

The responsibility for making things happen in a company lies with the managing director and his senior managers. In hard times businesses are susceptible to crises of different orders of magnitude and importance than those which occur in good times. Surviving difficulties requires a knowledge of cash flow and an ability to change direction, to respond flexibly to the market and to customers' needs. Bank managers may not be relaxed about overdraft facilities, and cost control becomes an even more important area of management concentration.

Improve cost controls

'What you measure you can control' is a very old work-study concept. A more modern and sharper version of this by the president of A.B. Electrolux is the title of a book on quality improvement: *What gets measured gets done.*

Knowing your costs is *the* key to profit improvement. Without non-subjective indicators of sales, performance, stock, costs profit by product, and so on, you will not know whether you are sinking or swimming. Do you know definitively what is happening in your company, or is cost control a contradiction in terms? It is a business motto that you can make a loss several times and still survive – but you can only run out of money once!

I have installed labour cost control schemes which have been based on a crudely established measurement of current output. However, by 'freezing' such standards they provided the necessary consistency to allow the plotting of a trend of improvement from an established baseline. Thus it was possible to measure increased productivity relatively and to pay for such increase with the knowledge that it had been achieved.

Such roughly established measurements of performance are useful whenever you want to establish control in the short term. They are a practical means of establishing non-subjective indications of productivity while better engineered standards and control systems are being introduced.

Another very useful control system is the profit and loss account, especially if you produce monthly management accounts. The consistency with which the accounting routines use data month after month should allow you to use the gross profit figure for an indication of manufacturing efficiency and the net profit figure to indicate the level of control on general expenditure.

Such indicators as growth, profit, turnover, inventory value, product costs, market share, and so on, are necessary if you are to know whether your cost-reduction programme is successful or not.

Keep it simple, stupid

Complexity costs money. The simple approach will bring dividends in areas of cost control in the company.

In the standardization of products

- Sony Walkman reduced 60 assembly operators to 49 and sales price from $38 to $33 by standardization of parts.
- Major motor manufacturers spend 30 per cent of development time in accounting for changes.
- One of our clients making woodworking machinery launched a new range, using standard modules for bases, tables, motors, and so on. The result is less cost because they can make bigger batches and need to stock fewer different parts. Maintenance is less complex and servicing is cheaper.

Simple production control

The JIT approach requires that we do not complicate the process any more than is absolutely necessary. We should not add to the complexity of control by working around a problem – we should solve it!

When a Japanese firm took over an American electronics company, the new managers simply told assembly workers not to pass on anything faulty – so they didn't. Initially, output plummeted as the line stopped whenever anyone spotted a fault. Management concentrated on sorting out the problems which stopped the lines, and within days the quality improved and output increased above previous levels because of a lower reject rate.

Simple communications

I was very impressed with a Yorkshire toolmaking company I visited in 1990. They make repeat tools for different customers. They have posted up what they call 'works instructions' which define the essential differences each customer needs on a particular mould, an easy, simple form of communication. On

60

the operation sheets they list out in simple everyday words the things to look for when doing each operation, such as that the leading edge must be machined and measured *before* the outside diameter.

All simple, easy to understand, clear instructions.

Simple measurement

Measurement may not need to be the most sophisticated. I remember a small company which was struggling to administer a detailed labour cost control scheme. This scheme required production workers to fill in time sheets and job cards and management to do a detailed analysis of each. The detail of analysis work was too time-consuming for a small company and was frequently not done because of other pressing work. By using 'chunkier' units of measurement for each department, for example total output in labour hours divided by total attendance time, management were able to plot the trend of productivity with ease and to establish whether performance was improving or not.

Set your sights higher

You should always plan for and expect increases in productivity. According to a survey by the CBI, the average British company expects increases of productivity of about 3 per cent per annum, yet my experience leads me to believe that the potential for increase is at least double management's estimate in most companies. However, even this modest improvement would result in a profit increase of 27 per cent in a typical company.

If you believe that quantum leap improvements are not possible in established businesses then you should hear about BICC, the international cable-making company. A 20 per cent per annum improvement in productivity has been achieved over the past three years through intensified attacks on costs. This well-controlled group with a reputation for good industrial engineering, production engineering, and manufacturing competence, after holding up well in the 1980s, began the 1990s with an enthusiasm for even higher levels of productivity. As cable-making employs fairly basic technology, these improvements have been done by producing quality goods at least cost. If BICC can achieve this level of year-on-year cost improvement, what prizes await other UK companies that do not start from such a high productivity base?

Dr Barry Dale, director of UMIST Quality Management Centre, after studying Japanese companies at first hand, said 'All the evidence from Japanese companies is that improvement targets act as key motivators.'

Sir John Harvey-Jones of 'Troubleshooter' fame is another person who believes that quantum leaps in productivity or cost reduction are possible in companies. He has called for sweeping management cuts at the BBC and describes the Corporation's attempt to make cuts of 5–10 per cent as nonsense. Sir John believes that the Corporation should be able to reduce costs by one third!

Does it earn its keep?

In Japan, Toyota Motors, the largest car maker, ordered its managers to cut office expenses by 10 per cent because of the deceleration in economic growth in 1991. The move included curbs on travel, entertainment, and other expenses not directly related to production or salaries.

There are a number of questions that you should ask yourself.

- Are all your cost centres necessary?
- Is all the cost essential?
- Do you measure the cost of non-added value services?
- What does not add value to the product? This list could include the following:

    packaging;
    transport, including company cars;
    travel and accommodation;
    advertising;
    telephones;

postage;
insurance;
carriage costs;
computers and office machinery (fax, copiers, etc);
office rent, rates;
lighting and heating;
stationery and printing;
energy costs;
entertaining.

Look at the costs critically at least annually. Budget to reduce them relative to turnover. If you cannot reduce these costs by 3 per cent per annum you are not doing your job properly. A 3 per cent cut in overheads could improve profit by up to 10 per cent.

Can you afford this department?

Many companies run specialized departments which are hardly justified from a strategic point of view and not justified at all from the perspective of cost considerations. Such departments might include toolroom, paint shops, heat treatment, transport, and design. Sometimes these departments have a historical background or they are activities close to the heart of the owners or directors.

An engineering company had a modern, well-equipped toolroom which was an indulgence by the chairman and the production director, both of whom were engineers. The company got into trading difficulties and had to make savings, so the toolroom was closed down and the plant sold off. The company was then able to subcontract its toolmaking requirements and to establish better cost control over tool design and repair.

Another company in the coach-building business had a paint shop to finish off the vehicles in house. This is a specialized job requiring separate facilities and stringent health and safety regulations, and the shop also took up a lot of much needed stores space. They now subcontract the painting; they determine the quality (because they are the customers); they have

63

more space for a 'closed stores'; and they make a profit on the paint work!

We deliver faster

The longer you carry the cost of your goods and services the more it costs you. As we have seen, one way of reducing this cost is by invoicing earlier. Another way is to buy later, and yet another way is to do the job quicker.

Many companies spread their resources, both people and plant, across many jobs, which produces a longer production cycle with a great deal of work in progress. If you can concentrate on fewer jobs then the same resources will complete them in fewer days. This means that you can order material or other purchases later, and you can finish the job earlier and invoice earlier. Each day by which you reduce the production cycle is as profitable as reducing a debtor day.

Dexion Ltd has a full-time short-cycle manager. It uses JIT techniques to minimize the time between receiving a customer's order and receiving his cash. In two years stock turnround improved from four times a year to ten times, and £10m stock reduced to £5.1m.

You should remember that for every £1m of turnover an increase of stock turnover from four to ten times a year will produce £67 500 better cash flow.

Telephone costs and uses

The Bank of America announced that a new system of telephone costs accountability was to be implemented within three months whereby departmental heads were responsible for budgets for telephone costs. Calls were to be monitored and non-business calls charged to each manager. Before the system was implemented, telephone costs were reduced by over 30 per cent!

Research has shown that 70 per cent of telephone calls are 'one way' in that there is no need for any discussion. On such occasions the phone may be inappropriate and a short fax or telex might be more apt.

On average, half the telephone calls made fail to result in a conversation simply because the person being called is away from the phone. So anticipate the possibility that the person you want to speak to may not be there, and be prepared to leave a succinct message which will save your telephone time yet still provide full and clear information about your call.

The National Audit Office reported in 1991 that the National Health Service could save up to 30 per cent of telephone calls, which would amount to £30m a year! Some hospitals were paying for lines they could not identify or which were being used by private subcontractors. Private calls and direct lines for senior staff were highlighted as being responsible for some hospitals having telephone bills 250 per cent higher than others.

Telephones are disruptive, and it is claimed that they are blamed for some very low white-collar worker productivity. It takes twenty-five minutes of quiet for some levels of concentration to be reached and, on this basis, two calls an hour can make a person who needs to concentrate virtually unproductive. The temptation is to leave the telephone off the hook, but this will only annoy the caller who wants to leave an urgent message. It is much better to divert the phone to a secretary or colleague who can take messages.

A fax machine is now an essential part of office equipment and customers expect to be able to contact you this way. The cost of sending a fax can be cheaper than a telephone call and, like the phone, there is a cheap fax rate.

You may find these tips on reducing telephone costs useful:

- do not accept reverse-charge calls – get your telephonist to call back;
- limit out-of-hours direct lines;
- telex and fax are cheaper, especially as they can be sent after 6 p.m.
- ask yourself if you need all your phones.

5

TWENTY-FIVE WAYS TO INCREASE REVENUE

It is well known that reducing costs is only one way to protect profits, and that the level of profitability can also be improved by higher income. Although I have devoted a lot of space to the cost-reduction avenue to better profit, some of the ideas in this chapter are pure profit opportunities. Any method of simple price increase (that is, without any accompanying added costs) is an easier way to profitability than any other in this book.

The setting of the price of the product or service is the least professional activity in many UK companies. It is often set by the salesman or the estimator – I even know of an engineering subcontractor where the price is set by the foreman of the department doing the work. Even when the price is determined by a suitably responsible person, there is often an alarming lack of costs knowledge and market awareness. There is probably as much potential improvement in company profitability from the setting of the optimum price as from any other source.

Marketing

Although the exact nature of marketing is quite hard to define it is an activity which most individuals do every day. People dress up to make themselves presentable or attractive; to make others aware of them; to hope others are going to like them. Business marketing is somewhat more structured (we hope) but the point of it all is very much the same.

Know the market-place

It might sound outrageous to suggest that companies do not know which market they are in, but I have seen enough examples to suggest that it may be true.

For years Dunlopillo, the bedding manufacturer, produced what it thought the customer wanted: a basic polyurethane mattress at the cheapest price. Yet, increasingly, management felt this was wrong; they had no real presence in mass-marketing, where sales were made on price alone, but had a strong brand based on quality. In the late 1980s, in spite of the falling demand in the furnishing industry, Dunlopillo raised its prices and continued to hold them even in the recession. They redesigned their range to make it even more luxurious and raised the prices another notch. The over-50s are now a prime market segment, for these 'grey' consumers have significant disposable income and will sometimes buy beds costing up to £4000 each.

Knowledge of the market-place might be quite a complicated subject in your business, but without it you are trading blind. I know a company which finds out what the local market will stand, and sets prices accordingly – but always below the competition. One of our clients in the packaging business has market research carried out for them about every three years. It helps to identify new growth industries which may use packaging, and any trends in packaging which might destroy some of their business, such as plastic or paper containers instead of glass.

Use your salesmen to collect market information – they are, after all, closer to the customer. Does your product fit the market? Can it be changed subtly and inexpensively to hit the market need accurately? Know what your customers will pay and what your competitors are charging.

All of this is helpful in enabling you to arrive at the optimum price. It is the opposite to cost reduction but has the same effect of increasing profit.

Wickes plc, the DIY merchant, has chalked up a remarkable record of growth in revenue and earnings in the past, doing all the wrong things! Most DIY chains – B & Q, Texas, Homebase, and so on – have 20 000 stock items. Wickes carry only 3500–4000 of the dullest, low-margin DIY range of goods, such as cement, bricks, and timber. Dick Clark, the MD, recalls the theory of the bumblebee which aerodynamically has a body weight too big for its wings (in theory it shouldn't be able to fly) and similarly, the last thing one should do in DIY is sell low-value products on high-cost land. There are, however, essentially three factors which account for Wickes's success: (*a*) their narrow range allows very favourable buying terms; (*b*) Wickes is the only name on display; and (*c*) approximately 25 per cent of customers are tradesmen who come, not to browse, but to buy.

How much is your product worth?

> Nothing is intrinsically valuable; the value of everything is attributed to it, assigned to it from outside the thing itself, by people.
>
> John Barth

Your product is worth what your customer will pay for it. Do you know what that is? Do you know the perceived value of your goods?

People do not buy on price alone (how many company car owners drive a Skoda?). In a recent survey, price was ranked behind quality, delivery, service, innovation, and customer care, as key factors when buying.

Is your product or service distinctive? If so, people will pay more for it. These companies have such a reputation: Marks & Spencer (goods can be returned for any valid reason); SAS

Hotels ('no excuses' – if anything goes wrong, no bill); Federal Express (trace a parcel in thirty minutes or no charge).

Do you include free of charge something in your service which the customer prizes enough to pay for? Many companies offer advice as a free service, such as kitchen designers, printers, tile shops, garden centres, and consultants of various kinds. Is your customer-care programme valued enough for your customer to buy from you regardless of price?

After a seminar at which I had spoken on ways to increase revenue, the managing director of a company making indus-trial shelving confided in me that he had confirmation only that day that he was guilty of not charging enough. A buyer, for whom he had produced a special set of shelving in double-quick time, told him that he should have charged more!

How would customers describe your product?

- Best;
- Value for money;
- Immediate delivery;
- Good value;
- Essential;
- Good after-sales support.

By the way – there is no point in being the cheapest or best or most reliable if nobody knows! *Tell them how good you are.*

I know of one company which makes farm machinery. Although they sold a good number of machines, very few farmers had been persuaded to take out maintenance contracts, yet the company provided a virtual 24-hour 'hot-line' with telephone diagnosis and fast response to breakdowns – at its own expense. After creating a service department and strongly marketing a priority service for customers taking out annual service contracts, advance premiums are now paying for the 'hot-line' and other service department expenses.

National Breakdown, the UK's third-largest motoring organi-zation, was also guilty of underpricing its service when it started in 1971. Ernest Smith, the managing director, recalls that the premium of £2 per year was simply not enough. It gave the new company no credibility, as people did not believe it would be able to provide a national recovery service at that price. 'If we had charged £10 we would have had a lot more members,' said Mr Smith.

Use your initiative

Instead of waiting for sales orders to come to you, why not make proposals to your customers? Why not research a potential customer's needs and create a proposal for a specific service to that customer? Make an appointment, present the customer with samples, ideas, and costs, and put forward ways in which he can use your service.

Victor Kiam, of Remington Razor fame, tells the story of a young woman employee who joined a department brainstorming session. She told the group of her recent experience in hospital where, as part of the pre-operation procedure, she had to be shaved. The nurse nicked her, only slightly, but it was enough for them to postpone the operation. She asked whether Remington could design an electric razor for hospitals. They could. The hospitals use only one razor, but with a disposable head for each patient. The company is now selling over three million heads each year.

Can you give away a 'loss leader' – a free survey, or a half-price first order? How about attempting to do those difficult jobs which companies shy away from in good times – the chances are you will not have too much competition to contend with.

Industrial Clothing Service (ICS) was in garment cleaning when it hit on an idea to clean and recondition industrial gloves – one Talbot factory alone used 15 000 pairs a week! ICS cut the cost of these consumables at Linwood by 50 per cent. Think how it would be if you could go to Ford and say 'I can save you a million pounds a year!'

Repackage your products

Repackage your products into other units which will increase your sales. One of the prime examples of this is that you can no longer buy a single screw or hinge at a DIY store – you have to buy a packet. This is an example of the manufacturer taking advantage of the means of retailing to sell more or at better prices.

Changes in legislation or standards can frequently offer the opportunity to change packaging to your advantage. The distilling industry has discovered that EC harmonization rules can be useful in changing buying habits. European Commission rules on whisky bottles were anticipated by the Scotch whisky distillers who switched from 75 centilitre to 70 centilitre bottles eight months before the deadline. The change represents a 7 per cent reduction in contents, and the distillers cut the price for the new bottle by 4 per cent.

Good advertising can be expensive ...

... but bad advertising is even dearer. Monitor your advertising results carefully; try to reduce the cost of comparable mailshots or advertisements and see if there is any reduction in the response. Do 'piggy-back' advertising or share the cost of an exhibition stand with a larger company or a non-competitive product.

See if you can do your own copywriting – we do. We also place job advertisements direct with newspapers and save the agent's fee. It might be more effective to employ a freelance journalist to send regular items to trade papers. Pay him on a no publish–no fee basis.

If you want to know how effective it would be to advertise in a newspaper, trade paper, or magazine, ask the other companies who already advertise there. They will tell you unless you are a competitor. Take the sales director out to lunch – a fifty-pound investment that could save or make you thousands.

Some time ago I used to pass a farm in Essex which sold produce to the passing public. I was always amused, and still am twenty years later, at the hand-written notice which said 'Farm eggs – laid while you wait.' Not expensive, but marvellously effective.

Advertising could change your business out of all recognition – like Bernard Matthews, who claims that the way he said 'bootiful' caught the imagination of the TV public and led to a 500 per cent growth in the business over ten years.

> *Half the money spent by our company on advertising is wasted. The problem is to find out which half.*
> Lord Leverhume

Selling

Selling is not the same as marketing, but is the important bit of it, the point of it all. It is the selling of the products that creates the income.

Salesmen need targets

The salesmen of a wholesale distribution company were required to visit every customer once a month yet, despite this high level of customer attention, the company was losing market share and reported losses over several years. The trouble was that 80 per cent of the salesmen's time was spent with customers whose business with the company was so small it could not cover the cost of the salesmen's calls.

You may well find, like other companies, that all your profits come from 20 per cent or 30 per cent of your customers. Examine your customer contribution. You might do better to have your salesmen visit your profit-contributing customers more frequently or to spend time processing their orders accurately.

Control your salesforce:

- set targets for them and make sure they know how they will be measured;
- monitor progress by producing regular actual versus budget figures;

- reward well, and relate the bonus to the effort required; if your bonus scheme is well controlled, do not stint on the reward – it will be coming out of increased profit;
- train (or replace); motivate your sales team with professional training, have your sales managers/director spend time with them on the road, and give them a chance to prove themselves.

If training, incentives, or encouragement do not succeed, then find another salesman.

If you monitor your salesmen's performances and you target to bring the below-average people up to the average, you could improve turnover by 20 per cent. Define the specific training each one needs and provide it, and you will be surprised at how easy it is to increase sales.

'Piggy-back' selling

Sell your products as a package with other suppliers, as many other companies already do:

- a free packet of Persil goes with every new washing machine;
- computer accessory supplies may be included in the initial order for hardware and software;
- some major industrial groups are taking the products of smaller companies into export markets, which gives the opportunity for joint advertising;
- tyres, lights, spark plugs, pumps, suspension kits, and so on, are old forms of piggy-back selling.

Can you sell via different outlets, such as wholesalers, mail order, house to house, or factory to factory?

Customer-sourced leads

Hard times do not allow the time-scale necessary to develop new customers from cold selling, especially when their current suppliers will be working hard to keep the business. So you have to find ways to shorten the selling time-scale. Finding a point of contact will do just that.

Your customers are not just any point of contact but a qualified reference of your service. Their opinion will carry weight with their contacts, so you need not only an introduction but, better still, a recommendation.

Some ways in which customers can help are:

- by providing a list of companies in their industry;
- by an introduction to members of their trade association (if there is one);
- even giving you copies of their trade magazine will help to identify potential customers.

I remember talking at a trade association meeting which led to a very long consultancy job with two of the companies attending. In consultancy, probably because of the personal nature of the relationship, clients often pass names to one another. Such qualified recommendation leaves very little selling to do.

If you sell widely used commercial products in stationery or motor cars or food or clothing, then *all* your customers have contacts who buy your products.

How to get bigger orders

Give discounts on a sliding scale relative to the quantities ordered. This may encourage customers, particularly at period end, to order more to qualify for the next level of discount. Help customers to give you bigger orders by showing them the rate card with the savings from larger orders. The advantage of ordering to the next level of discount will be the benefit you will be pointing up.

The sale of accessories can be a way to increase the size of an order. They are add ons, they are desirable, and they enhance the purchase already made. Take the computer salesman who, after selling, will find an opportunity to sell a back-up cartridge to save half an hour at the end of each day for the customer;

or a single sheet feeder for mailshots;
or mail-merge software;
or a modem so that their salesman can enter orders overnight;
or a laser printer;
or an additional terminal;
or extra memory.

Pay for sales leads

Encourage everyone in your company who comes in contact
with the customer to sell to him. Service engineers, drivers,
credit controllers, and telephonists all have the opportunity to
bring up the subject of customer satisfaction. They do not have
to sell, but they should be able to recognize a buying signal. If
you really want to motivate them, pay them for any leads
which result in sales. My company does not have salesmen/
women, because we believe that it is probably easier to train
operational staff to sell a service (or product) than to train
salesmen to do the work.

When I ran a computer software consultancy we employed a
brilliant programmer who could almost make a computer sit up
and beg. Like many technically-biased people, he preferred
machines to people and was never happier than when he was
'inside' a machine. Although he was a one-track-minded
technician, our customers loved him – he was sometimes rude,
never suffered fools, and was generally antisocial, but because
he was only interested in technology his outspokeness was
seen as unbiased comment on either system hardware or
software, and was seen as having no selling bias. We received a
lot of work as a result of his strange relationship with our
customers.

Turn more enquiries into sales

I have known companies who receive so many enquiries that
they do not reply to them all. That always seems to me to be
nothing less than criminal.

Even in difficult times, in some businesses the rate of enquiries can increase, either because competitors go out of business and their customers need a new supplier, or simply because the buyer wants competitive quotations from other companies. If you are in this fortunate position then you should streamline your estimating procedures. Computerized estimating programmes can increase the output of an estimator by a factor of ten. Of the quotations which you do complete, do you know how many you convert into sales? Can you improve this ratio? For example: if you can change a 10:1 enquiry conversion ratio to 9:1 you will increase sales by 11 per cent.

Sell on your experience, your success, your track record, and references from satisfied customers – other people do – and if your product has helped other companies in similar businesses, say so.

If your quotation is not successful, find out why. Ask the customer. It will not only help you to get it right next time, but it gives you another opportunity to discuss the sale with the buyer.

At the enquiry stage you are so close to a sale – you have a buyer who wants your product and who wants it now – that it is worth spending time and effort in closing this sale. Better-quality response to enquiries and/or invitations to tender will have proportionately better results than almost any other activity.

Pricing

Although the cost of a product has some part to play in the determination of the selling price, there is no direct relationship between the two. Many companies calculate a price by a predetermined margin of profit added to costs, but this can either produce a price that is unacceptably high to the customer, or produce lower profit than it might.

Recession times are difficult ones for price-setting, and the tendency is to lower prices to keep business. It is preferable for company profitability to keep prices high and give better service, training, delivery, choice, or other concessions not price-associated.

Put up the price

What effect on profit would a 1 per cent increase in prices have? Although in some businesses it might be difficult to put up the price by even this small amount if the competition is very fierce, there are many businesses where this level of increase would go unnoticed. Yet a 1 per cent increase in prices could improve net profit by 10 per cent. Even in a very competitive market the other benefits of buying from you, like service, quality, and timely delivery, should easily justify a 1 per cent difference in price.

Some companies have difficulty in raising prices and 'selling' the increases to customers. If you find that you need to increase revenue part way through a financial year, there is no merit in waiting to run out of cash or out of business. Your task is to persuade customers to accept other than annual increases:

- warn the customer in advance to give him the chance to buy at current prices;
- use the opportunity to market new products or sell old stock or to keep production running out of season.

I know a man who runs a business selling textiles. From time to time he instructs his sales people to add another 1p to the cost per metre. With his turnover, each penny adds £30 000 to his income. A 1p rise every three months is better than a 4p rise at the end of the year!

If you are anxious about the effect of raising prices, then start selectively. Introduce new prices to certain customers or industries or regional locations.

Discounting

This is a very useful selling aid but it should be controlled. Negotiators should know the true product costs so that they do not sell at a loss – except for strategic reasons, which will be at the discretion of management.

Quantity discounts: how often do you give the discounts, even on orders which do not qualify by volume?

Settlement discounts: how often do you forget to enforce the settlement period? There is no use giving 2.5 per cent discount to a customer who normally pays within thirty days!

Seasonal discounts: make sure that orders do not spill over into your busy periods – the discount should be of benefit to you when things are slack.

Discounting is a management tool and should be used positively to:

- even out capacity demands (see the section 'Think Bottlenecks' in Chapter 4, p.56);
- keep good customers;
- resist market share deterioration;
- act as loss leaders.

Do not, however, give discounts without any good reason. Control your discounting – never let your salesmen discount without a trade-off, such as bigger orders or earlier payment.

Discounting can be a good way to move obsolete or redundant stock. If it is material or stock which is out-of-date or has been superseded, then the longer you hold it the less valuable it will be. It is better to have the cash equivalent of even the lower realizable value in your current account.

Discounting can be a powerful selling tool – as Peter Drucker has written, 'No customer loyalty can survive a 2 per cent discount'.

Minimum order quantities

The last time I saw some figures published about the cost of raising an invoice, it was £25 – it may now be double that. Even if it is only £30, the sales value of the order must be at least £100 just to contribute to overheads. If the debt is outstanding for sixty days, and if it requires any credit control attention, then the sale will have made a loss.

Orders involving any specialist time, such as design, delivery, estimating, buying, and so on, will add to the share of overheads which the order must bear to be profitable. Your pricing policy must be flexible enough for you to recover the cost of administration, management, or specialist time, but you have to know the cost in order to operate a flexible pricing policy.

Allow for cash with order or use a simple sales invoice for small orders, and build into your estimating routine an opportunity to charge extra for recognizable additional costs.

Point up the benefits

In a competitive tendering situation, it is important for your customers to compare like with like. Itemize all the important constituent parts of a job, separating the common from the distinctive service which you provide. It will help you to point up the superiority of your product or service and will justify your price, if that becomes an issue. List all the product features and their benefit to the user, and make sure they are included somewhere in your tender document or proposal.

If you have British Standard 5750 quality control certification, or the Queen's Award for Industry, or 'blue chip' customers, or new processes, or latest technological processes, and so forth, your customers should know. How else can they differentiate between the best and the rest?

Charge for extras

This follows on from the previous point, but is different in some respects. The former justifies the price for the standard product; this is to let the customer know that he can have what he wants, but at a cost.

If your customer requires extras which were not covered in your original price, you must tell him at the time. Point out that you can paint it in metallic paint or put bigger wheels on, hinge it at the back instead of the front, but that it will cost more. It is the difference between a businessman's lunch and à la carte:

79

one can cost £5 and the other whatever is your expense account limit.

If your customer wants express or overnight delivery, make sure he knows that it will cost more. There is nothing more frustrating to your people than a job well done and delivered quickly to help out a customer, only for the customer to complain about the price.

I once saw a sign over a greengrocer's stall which could hardly be bettered as a summary of this section:

Grapefruit

Our Choice	...	40p
Your Choice	...	50p

Customers

A patient to a doctor
A guest to the hotelier
A client to the solicitor
A subscriber to the publisher
A shopper to the retailer
A passenger to the airline
A voter to the politician
A student to the professor
A customer by any other name ...

There is pinned to a drawer of my desk a tattered cutting from a magazine which reads: 'The object of a business is *not* to make money – it is to serve customers. The result is to make money.' I do not know who coined the phrase but, for me, it has served to make the distinction between the aims and the means.

Hundreds of new customers

Where will the average company find hundreds of businesses with whom it does business already, but who do not buy from it? The answer will be found in the purchase ledger.

Your suppliers represent an untapped list of businesses who could buy from you. If you make nuclear power plants or breed ferrets then this means of finding new customers will not apply to you, but in the majority of businesses at least some of the names in the purchase ledger will be buying what you sell.

In the case of a service industry company, almost all suppliers need the product at some time. If you are an accountant, *all* your suppliers need what you sell.

If you are a service industry, or supplying to the home, factory, shop, or office, or selling products or services aimed at individuals rather than companies or institutions, then some or all of your suppliers have either a corporate need or will employ people who have a need for what you sell.

Not only does this identify potential new customers, but they are companies with whom you already have contacts. It should be easy to get an appointment – after all, you are the customer! You talk to the people in these companies frequently, you write to them monthly (if only to send a cheque).

If you are a travel agent, imagine saying to your painter, or joiner, or car dealer, or solicitor, 'Your cheque's here – if you'd like to pick it up you can take away the latest holiday brochures.' This will be the friendliest potential customer you have ever spoken to – you are giving him money yet sowing the seeds of a sale at the same time.

Once a customer. always a customer

Statistics show that it is five times cheaper to retain a customer than obtain a new one. Stick close to the customer. You will not have to look for new customers if you look after the old ones.

People who have brought from you in the past are ideal sources of revenue increases because (*a*) they buy what you sell; (*b*) you can target selling time at them; and (*c*) you already have a personal contact with them.

Why not 'lock' the next sale into the last one? Can you give credit or vouchers towards the next purchase? I read of a photographic laboratory which gives credit vouchers for exposures which do not come out; the clever thing is, they give credits for lost exposures even when there is none! I often think that garages which service cars have a great opportunity to sell on, with reminders for the next service, new accessories, next model, and the like. If you sell to the home, can your product fit the office, or vice versa?

- Put the customer first. He is king – without him you don't have a business.
- Put yourself in his place. See the problem from where he sits. Solve his problems and you have a customer for life.
- Think like him. What are his needs? How can your product satisfy him?
- Keep in touch. Find any excuse to make contact to introduce a new product, to inform on new prices, or to meet a new sales representative.
- Know about any staff changes, particularly in the purchasing department.
- Listen to him. Remember what Lyndon B. Johnson said: 'You ain't learnin' nothin' when you're talkin.'

Hundreds of potential customers

Your employees may come in contact with lots of potential users of your products. Your suppliers could be customers (see 'Hundreds of new customers' above). Job applicants could be customers. People who leave your employment could be customers. Accountants do a lot of business with people who trained with the company and who subsequently become financial directors.

Visiting salesmen are worth cultivating. They go into lots of companies; have lots of contacts; know a lot about how companies are trading. They love talking to people, especially potential customers like you.

What about having a good chat with your bank manager? He knows all about local companies, and will often effect an introduction where there is mutual advantage. Even management consultants can provide you with customers: I have put buyers and sellers together in packaging, electronics, steel supplies, and many other areas of business.

Other people who could introduce new customers include your professional advisers – accountant, solicitor, insurance broker, Rotary club contacts – and attendees at conferences, seminars, or trade show exhibitions.

What else does the customer need?

- Lever Brothers now sells a Persil washing-up liquid;
- Milkmen sell potatoes, eggs, fruit squash, and so on;
- Shops sell carrier bags in which to carry the goods home;
- Accountants sell consultancy services;
- Software houses sell hardware;
- Estate agents sell house insurance.

You should think about selling existing products to new customers – or new products to old customers – or new products to new customers.

H. Fine & Son provides low-tech bits and pieces for armies, like covers for guns and radar equipment, canvas toolbags, muzzles for mortars, even bulletproof vests. They have now added a folding ladder to the range, but a folding ladder with a difference. It folds to the size of a two-litre Coca-Cola bottle, yet extends to twelve feet – ideal for the defence and security industries.

Kelloggs is spending a small fortune on television advertisements for its cornflakes aimed at changing our eating habits – to convert people to eat breakfast cereals at night!

Can your salesman carry other products which may be complementary but not competitive? Alternatively, it might be to your advantage to have your salesman carry the goods of other companies and to make reciprocal arrangements for their salesman to carry your goods, on the basis that when times are hard you should actually increase the sales effort, not reduce it.

Selling to someone else's customers

When you want good ideas about how to survive or even grow in a recession, look at the way that the best people in your market go about it.

The success of Cramphorn plc is a great example to companies in the retail sector. In the five years to 1990, despite having a slightly lower turnover than the previous five years, at about £15m, pre-tax profits have grown from £0.5m to £1.34m. This company, which operates a number of garden centres, is a good example of how to make money out of complementary products without the associated costs. Rather than diversify itself, it has invited concessionaires selling anything from pools to pet foods to craft items. These concessionaires are responsible for their own stock and their own staff and rent space from Cramphorn, who receive £400 000 from concession income alone. They also get the added bonus of increased customer flow.

This increase in business was also experienced by a builders' merchant who was anxious about the effect on trade from a B & Q store which opened across the road from him. He need not have worried. Serious DIY builders park their cars on the B & Q car park and flock to his yard to buy their building materials, or call in after their visit to the superstore. Some Sunday mornings there is even a queue of cars waiting for his gates to open.

Revenue from non-products

In difficult times, it might be possible to increase income from non-product sources. Income could be generated by an asset clearance sale, by rental from the sub-let of premises, by selling your experience (consultancy), or by selling equity in the company.

The use of non-productive assets or stock which is not moving in order to generate cash is an idea that management could pursue. The use of assets as security for temporary borrowing is something that should be considered earlier rather than later, particularly if the material or products which are used as security are items that will sell in normal trading times.

Production machinery which is inefficient, surplus to requirements, out-of-date, or redundant to the company's current or future needs, is a useful source of additional income. This has the same effect as a cost-reduction operation, namely, that it creates more cash, although it does not appear on the profit and loss account and is a balance-sheet item. Examination of your machinery, buildings, plant, warehouse, and vehicles may show some items which are not necessary to your current operation, but would be of value to some other company.

Assets do not necessarily need to be sold off to generate additional cash. The sub-letting of buildings is a particular example of having an asset generate cash other than from the main activities of the company.

I know an ice-cream manufacturer who has spare capacity in his cold store in the winter and hires it out for Christmas fowl and other food in November and December. Even the subcontracting of people who have particular skills which other companies can use on a part-time or temporary basis is a potential source of short-term income. Computer programmers, service engineers, designers, and lorry drivers are among those jobs which it would be easy to find another company with whom to share costs.

When Tesco needed to keep up its growth in recessionary times, it found the necessary £500m not from the banks, which would have meant high interest costs, but by a rights issue of shares, with preference being given to existing shareholders.

6

POPULAR WAYS TO PUT UP PROFITS

Don't just aim to make improvements – fire!
D.L. Moody

Every company will have areas of relative inefficiency or out-of-controlness which will respond in its own way to investigation. In one company, it might be lower head office costs which provide the savings; in another, the realization that prices are too low which triggers revenue improvements; selling off an unused machine or vehicle could improve liquidity; completing jobs quicker might be the key to lower overheads; knowledge of profit contribution by customer or product might allow a company to cease supplying to poor contribution customers, leading to lower turnover but higher profits. It is hoped that the list of potential areas for improvement in Chapters 4 and 5 will be a useful reminder of dormant opportunities waiting to be rediscovered.

My own experience suggests that there are six areas of likely improvements which might apply in most companies. Although these will not all apply in any one company, they serve to illustrate the cumulative effect which a concentrated attack on key cost areas can have.

People
People productivity. It is likely that measurement, motivation, target-setting, and labour-cost controls will produce a 10 per cent reduction in unit labour cost.
Improvement potential: 10%   *Net effect on profit:* 2%

86

Materials
Reduced inventory and better buying. The likely potential improvement from good management of stocks, investigations into materials and components bought and used in products, and the determined effort to secure a lower price from suppliers should provide a 5 per cent reduction in materials used.
Improvement potential: 5%   *Net effect on profit: 2.5%*

Liquidity
Improved cash control. A professional approach to debt collection and creating a balance between creditor and debtor lists should result in an improvement in funds equal to 10 days' earlier collection of sales invoices.
 Improvement potential: 10 days   *Net effect on liquidity: 3%*

Organization
Reduced job cycle. With better production planning and control, it ought to be possible to reduce the time it takes to deliver a job by the equivalent of one week over a year. This will be equal to 2 per cent better throughout and one week's better cash flow.
Improvement potential: 1 week   *Net effect on liquidity: 2%*

Pricing
Wider profit margins should be possible by better knowledge of product costing and customers' awareness of the value of products. A 2 per cent increase in prices will drop to net profit.
 Improvement potential: 2%   *Net effect on profit: 2%*

Costing/selling
Improvement in conversion of sales leads. When customers are asking you to quote prices for jobs, you are as near to a sale as you can get. Increased effort at this stage by attention to detail and discussion of exact needs with the customer will be more beneficial than spending time elsewhere. A 5 per cent better sales conversion will result in probably 2 per cent better profits.
 Improvement potential: 5%   *Net effect on profit: 2%*

If profit is a nominal 10 per cent, then this programme of improvement will increase that by 85 per cent and produce additional cash equal to 5 per cent of turnover.

Not all of this improvement is ongoing because any inventory reduction is a once-off saving, although there is, of course, the saving in interest on reduced borrowings. On the other hand, cost reductions from people performance, reduction in job cycle, and cutting out unprofitable business are all repeat savings.

Table 4 is an actual list of profit-making calculations from several companies at a 'profit protection' workshop.

Table 4   Profit-making calculations

Company	Profit idea	Improvement	Effect on net profit
Contract cleaning	Better stock control	70%	Once-off savings equal to 140% of net profit plus equivalent of 23% p.a. savings in lower interest
Office stationery, equipment, and furniture	Target higher productivity from sales personnel	10%	90% plus
Day-care nursery group	Cost forecasting control	10–15%	100% plus
Cleaning services	Labour efficiency by better task setting and work recording	20%	More than 100% increase
Visual aids manufacturer	Better cash flow by matching debtors and creditors	3% lower costs	27% plus
Strapping systems supplier	Buy only what you need	4% lower costs	Once-off savings equal to 20% net profit plus 4% p.a. ongoing
Manufacturer of high-quality interior architecture	Know what your products are worth	8% higher prices	At least 100% increased profit

7

RECESSION TACTICS

It isn't important to come out on top; what matters is to come out alive.

Bertolt Brecht

Manage the situation

'To survive you must be ingenious, eccentric, different,' says Pat Grant of Norfrost. Pat and her husband, Alex, have created a remarkable company building freezers in the remotest part of northern Scotland against great odds. Pat Grant does the buying and drives a hard bargain in the purchase of materials and components. They buy at lowest cost with no gimmicks, no Christmas presents, no backhanders. The competition admit that their components cost more than the Norfrost selling prices. The Norfrost philosophy is that you start with no preconceived ideas about industry, you imitate no-one. The company is not an end in itself – it is a means to produce the best possible product at the best possible price.

Only numbers can provide objective measurement of business performance. Effective financial and operational management is required for profit protection and is the means to reduce unit costs. Careful scrutiny of accurate and up-to-date reports is necessary to determine remedial action. At the heart of any survival programme will be a sound financial and operational analysis of past performance, current results, and future trends. Understanding and 'owning' these figures is a vital prerequisite to profit improvement.

Financial management includes careful cash control and forecasting; appraising and controlling costs; and examining

89

and, if necessary, restructuring financial arrangements. Liquidity, customer awareness, cost control, and determination are the key success factors in hard times.

The objective of this chapter is to assist an organization to protect profits by concentrating on improving the performance of current resources. As Peter Drucker says, 'Making resources productive is the specific job of management' (*Managing in Turbulent Times*).

In order to do this, focus on the main resources of the organization:

* plant;
* finances;
* systems;
* human resources.

Let me illustrate this from the experience of a profitable company in the packaging business. One of their keys to good profits is very tight cost control. This company pays detailed attention to daily performances: they not only measure production at the end of each shift, they even have a 'half-time' score to record output after the morning shift.

Managing in a recession is all about being in control. If you are not in control, then get in control; if you are in control, then stay in control.

A sporting goods manufacturer had been in business for about sixteen years, grown at some 30 per cent per annum, and had a turnover of £4m. When one year sales did not materialize according to budget, the bank asked the company to reduce its overdraft which by then was over £1m. Without the bank's support, the company was in danger of going out of business. Management implemented short-term improvements to bring the company back into control. These included:

* consolidation of manufacturing facilities on a single site instead of several small units;
* introduction of material requirements planning;
* better stock control routines.

These short-term control initiatives produced a dramatic reduction in stockholding, clearer production requirements planning, early notice of purchasing requirements, ability to respond to customer requirements, and improved the company cash flow by £400 000.

Managing a company in a recession, indeed, survival, requires working hard at improving cash flow and remaining liquid, pushing costs down and controlling *all* expenditure very tightly, and keeping close to your customers and being twice as attentive to them as normal.

In order to manage the situation, set yourself short-term achievable goals and weekly, monthly, and quarterly targets. These should be not only achievable but simple in concept and understandable by your employees, such as:

- agree with suppliers to take five days longer credit;
- cut debtor days by five through better collection;
- reduce stocks by 5 per cent by using what is in stock;
- get one new customer per week.

Action speaks louder than words

Survival tactics are concerned with planning and activity in the short term. Do not expect things to get better tomorrow of their own accord – they probably won't. In tough times it is important to begin the process of survival early:

- to tighten spending;
- to create new trading opportunities;
- to detect warning signs in customers;
- to cut costs by higher efficiency;
- to release cash through lower inventory;
- to stay close to customers.

Rising material and production costs, increasing debtor days, and escalating overhead costs are just a few of the areas requiring constant monitoring.

Best courses of action will develop from:

- evaluating your current position;
- determining your competitive position;
- examining your product profitability;
- forecasting market trends;
- assessing your future direction.

One clue to better profits is to distinguish those products and services which generate profits from those which incur losses, and to draw up plans to concentrate on the winners.

In a recession, strategic management action must pay more attention to that most ignored resource – time. The time-scale of action is usually, necessarily, short. Managing in a recession is like being on a ship heading for an iceberg; you have to do three things, and quickly:

- stop it;
- turn it;
- head in the right direction.

Act early to stop the things which will sink the company. There will be no time for long-term strategy but a need for executives with ability to think quickly. This usually requires some risk-taking decisions but, faced with the alternative, doing nothing is not really an option.

Clear assessment of the situation is required. The aim of the assessment is to identify those aspects of the business operations which are important to survival. The emphasis will be on short-term rather than long-term activities and it will be important to examine the following:

- cash flow;
- profit and loss situation;
- organization and people;
- profits;
- market;
- control information;
- pricing policy;

- marketing and sales;
- internal cost controls.

It will be important to get the best available facts on all the above areas. Without good information a clear assessment is difficult, and without an ability to see the problem clearly the resultant executive action will be at best hopeful.

Stay in control

Ask yourself, could expenditure on inventory, long-term development, exotic marketing, and unnecessary overheads be reduced? Make every pound pay its way.

When expenditure is under control, then make reductions in unit labour costs and support costs by setting standards for higher efficiency. Target new levels of performance.

A company manufacturing car exhaust systems employed eighty people with a turnover of £3m. It had only basic systems of production control and labour-cost control, and was unable to identify shortcomings in work flow, materials handling, and machine efficiency and utilization. The benefits from improved control were calculated at about £100 000 in direct labour costs, with the same amount of savings accruing through additional overhead recovery.

Target-setting for direct operatives also increased performances by over 10 per cent, and the total benefits from improved control are now running at £300 000 p.a. on a £3m turnover.

Be liquid – stay liquid

All my available funds are completely tied up in ready cash.
W.C. Fields

One of the important survival techniques is expressed in the battle cry, 'Be liquid – stay liquid'. Even in good times, it is not unusual to find companies who have gone out of business with full order books, purely because they did not manage the cash flow.

When survival is the principal issue the priority is to keep lenders and creditors in place. Interest rates matter less than debt finance. As we have said elsewhere in this book, it is the lack of cash which provides the biggest threat to company survival. Although interest rates are high and some industries which have failed in the recent past have put the blame on high interest rates, it is the management of liquid assets which is more important.

Take a company with a turnover of £100m and costs of £90m. Costs per day will thus equal £250 000. I have known such companies go out of business for the sake of a lot less than £250 000, yet it is only equal to one day's better liquidity. In the case of a small company with a turnover of £1m, the daily cost of £2500 is just as likely to be unsupported by the local bank manager.

I have used a simple set of procedures with clients to ensure control of bank overdraft.

(1) First manage your debtors list more professionally. Apply the Pareto principle to all outstanding invoices. You will find that 80 per cent of the value is owed by less than 20 per cent of your customers. You should know their routines for paying invoices, and your credit controllers should be on speaking terms with the purchase ledger supervisor. Have your credit controller develop a forecast of payments against sales invoices, if this is not already done. Your credit controller will probably get this horribly wrong to begin with but will become more accurate with the predictions as time goes on.

(2) Have your purchase ledger supervisor produce a schedule of payments against your purchase invoices. Each week calculate the true overdraft statement and have the anticipated outgoing cheque payments listed for the following two weeks.

(3) Overlay the anticipated receipts of incoming cheques as determined by the credit controller on to the schedule of payments. This may indicate a shortfall of incoming cash relative to outgoings which would adversely affect the bank

overdraft. The size of such a shortfall then becomes the priority figure which the credit controller must get in from customers. Using a two-week time-scale it allows the credit controller to identify the most likely outstanding debtors which amount to at least the shortfall between expenditure and income, and to find ways of persuading the customers to pay up within the following seven days. In addition to the credit controller managing the debtor list by identifying priorities according to due date, size of debt, and amount outstanding, he will have a more sharply focused amount of money which the company needs to balance its cash flow. This action is repeated each week.

Be brave with prices

The most important managerial quality is courage.
Peter Drucker

Be brave with setting and maintaining your prices. Stay confident of the quality of your product or service. I know of companies in the 1991 recession that were offered discounts of 15 and 20 per cent by their suppliers, without even being asked! This kind of discounting madness will only accentuate cash-flow problems.

The managing director of one of our more profitable clients advises that companies who want to be profitable should know the true costs of the product in order to get the right price to earn them a decent profit. His dictum that 'You might as well play for nothing as work for nothing' is a fair statement of the alternative.

Running a business in tough times is not for the faint-hearted. It is a time for maintaining prices and even increasing them where possible. I have known companies who have cancelled special discounts to existing customers during lean times. Do not underestimate the value of your product or service, nor the need of your customers for a continuing supply of good-quality products. In recessionary times, you can always point to examples of other companies going out of business as a good reason for you to increase prices!

Do not unquestioningly accept the received wisdom of such common beliefs as:

- all UK goods are dearer than imported goods;
- you cannot sell electronic goods into Japan;
- you cannot get paid for goods before delivery;
- if you put your prices up, your customers will go elsewhere.

None of the above is necessarily correct, and there are instances where each of them is incorrect. So, make sure your product or service is first class and your customer satisfaction is second to none, then be brave with your prices.

Always remember the poster on the window of a discount store which read, 'We underprice everybody', which soon had another poster stuck on top of it reading, 'Closing Down Sale'.

Talk to everybody

When times are tough, this is one of the most important activities on which you should spend time. Talk to:

- suppliers;
- customers;
- bankers;
- employees;
- managers;
- competitors.

With the possible exception of the last category, the others all have one thing in common – they all want you to survive!

Suppliers

With suppliers, your problems are their problems. Your cut-back in production is their cut-back in sales. Your demise would mean that they would need to find another outlet for the level of business you do with them.

Why not ask your suppliers to reduce their prices to you during the hard times? In effect, you are asking them to share the downturn in profit which you are experiencing. That may be preferable to losing you as a customer.

Customers

Listen to customers – your survival should be important to them as an integral part of their own service to *their* customers. Ask them to give you more commitment to longer runs, or to provide material free of charge, or to pay bills earlier.

Listen to customers even when they complain. IBM talks about the 'joy of complaints'. For every customer who complains, fifty walk instead of complaining.

Keep close to them, satisfy them, make sure that your quality of product and level of service cannot be surpassed by any competitor. If you have the fastest delivery service, best-quality product, best after-sales service, lowest prices, or widest range, then tell them – how else will they know? Make sure you do not lose any existing business through negligence, apathy, underestimation of the competition, or ignorance. Whatever the level of existing customer orders, defend it against all comers.

When you have talked to your current customers, then talk to old customers, customers who have bought from you before but who do not currently do so. Tell them about your new levels of efficiency, wider range, lower costs, and so on.

Bankers

Talk to your bankers – they more than anyone will want you to succeed. Help them to support you by being forthright about your situation. They will want to help you, and you need to help them to relax about your trading condition. One bank manager blames company owners and directors for often making fundamental errors. 'When trading conditions deteriorate, customers fail to properly communicate their problems to us and are often not prepared to admit their failures,' he says. 'Too often, they cover up one mistake with another. They should be prepared to take the pain earlier rather than later. Sometimes, the first indication we have that something is wrong is when the overdraft limit is breached. Cheques start bouncing about, and we have to intervene and ask what is going on.'

Making sure that you fully understand the rules under which the local bank manager is currently lending is an important primary action in this game plan. Any changes in your indebtedness, borrowings, or cash flow, or any fall in the value of the bank security, such as property, or even a new bank regional policy on lending, may affect your business dramatically. So talk to your bank manager, keep him informed of your situation and, more importantly, your plans to survive.

Employees

Talk to employees – remember that your survival is their survival. Help them to have confidence in your leadership in these difficult times. Whenever a vacuum exists about the state of trading, or the liquidity of the company, or the size of the order book, then the 'grapevine' provides its own version of events. When rumours cause uncertainty, the people who first look for a new position are the employees you would not want to lose.

I once attended a client's board meeting and was pleasantly surprised to see on the agenda an item called 'Fighting The Recession'. It is important to face the facts squarely if a survival plan is to be successful, and the airing of recession problems certainly gave that company the opportunity to do something early.

Do not try to beat the recession on your own – share the problems with your managers and other employees. Build a winning team and make survival a team objective. Close ranks – you and your team – against the rest.

There is a motto in business that nothing succeeds better than success. When you have success in a particular area, either of cost reduction or of profit enhancement, or you have won back an old customer or received a big order, tell people in your company all about it. If there is a lack of information about how the company is going on it is just as likely to be filled with stories of doom and gloom as with stories of success. So beat the grapevine to it, shout out your successes as often and as loud as possible, and it could be the start of an upward cycle of fortune for your company.

Managers

Keep your managers informed – these are the people who have a considerable amount of influence on how you will survive. They are the decision-makers in their own area of responsibility. They will want to help out in a difficult situation, and will relish the opportunity to help you manage the company in difficult times – they are, after all, your *managers*, and you (presumably) employ them to manage. These are the people who are closest to the workforce, and their motivation is critically important.

Competitors

Talk to competitors – at the very least, this will enable you to confirm your judgement about the state of your own industry. You might also find out how they are dealing with the situation. If competitors are trading badly, it might indicate that they may not be a competitor of yours for very long. If they are riding the rough times well, you might be able to learn something from them.

During the desert campaign in the Second World War General Montgomery is said to have had a picture of the German Commander, General Rommel, hung in his head-quarters. I am not suggesting that you should request a picture of the chairman of your biggest competitor, but the more you know about them the less you are likely to be surprised at any of their actions in the market-place.

Customer care

Dissatisfied customers tell an average of twelve other people about it.

Manchester Business School

Using the 80:20 ratio rule, determine which 20 per cent of your customers represent 80 per cent of your profits. These are the companies you should stay close to, particularly in the short term. Your salesmen should visit these companies at the expense of other customers. Your managing director or sales director should find an opportunity to meet with directors or senior management or both in these key customer companies.

If you have a convenient reason for a meeting, like the launch of a new product or a reception to celebrate your achievement of BS5750 quality assurance, then fine, but you do not really need an excuse. If you are a prime supplier to a company then your interest in them and their need to trade current and future business plans is good commercial collaboration.

The advantages to you should be clear: an opportunity to learn at first hand of levels of trade and future business plans, an opportunity to identify areas of potential business, an opportunity to enhance your reputation with up-to-date reports on new developments and facilities within your company and, most importantly, the chance to reinforce your position as the prime source for the goods or services which you sell.

Super salesmen

You and your directors should spend time with your salesmen as they go around talking to your customers. Not only will this give the salesmen a reason for asking for a high-level meeting with a customer, but you will get the opportunity to see how the salesmen operate. Perhaps now is the time to give your sales force another injection of sales training. Despite all the education and publication of sales methods and techniques, it is still being said, by those in the selling profession who should know, that in two-thirds of all sales presentations the salesman forgets to ask for an order.

Tell them how good you are

One way to reinforce your customers' confidence in you is to tell them how good you are. Take a leaf out of the book of Tom Farmer of Kwik-Fit who regularly puts out advertisements for his products with the following endorsement: 'Our aim is 100 per cent customer satisfaction 100 per cent of the time.'

Know your customers

Tom Peters, in his book *A Passion for Excellence*, writes that the secret of success is not market, not marketing, not strategic positioning, but an obsession with customers.

Use everyone in your company to add to the sum total of your knowledge about the market-place and your customers. One of our clients has one of the most unusual newsletters I have ever seen. It consists mainly of cuttings from newspapers and trade periodicals which all the employees – salesmen, managers, printers, accounts people, drivers, and so forth – are encouraged to look out for and submit to the one person responsible for the newsletter. All the employees receive the newsletter, so the information in it about the state of the market or any particular customer is not isolated or restricted to the directors or the sales team. This open-handed attitude to the market-place encourages employees at all levels to add to their knowledge of the business world as it affects the company.

Be flexible

> *Consistency is contrary to nature, contrary to life. The only completely consistent people are dead.*
>
> Aldous Huxley

101

In times of uncertain sales and profits, the key word is flexibility. Radical thinking calls for:

- flexible cost structures;
- flexible cash flow through reduced overheads;
- flexible inventories;
- flexible production cycles.

Even the mighty change the rules in tough times. I was interested in the change in practice announced by the Walt Disney organization, which opened a store in Regent Street in 1990. They have a reputation of sticking to their prices – 'We will never have a sale' was a training course motto – but in January 1991 the price of some of the goods was halved!

To illustrate the point further, let me recall the story of the man who was building an extension to his house. He went to Magnet Joinery and ordered £2000 worth of doors, windows, and floorboards. Some months previously this man had been a victim of the Queensway furniture crash when he ordered and paid for a three-piece suite which he did not receive. When Magnet Joinery asked for payment in advance, the customer was anxious not to be caught again, so offered a postdated cheque or alternatively payment to the driver on delivery. The salesman was not able to accept this form of payment but he offered the customer free credit for three months, courtesy of a High Street Bank! I cannot believe that this company was unable to find some way of taking a customer's money.

Be ingenious

The secret of business is to know something that nobody else knows.

Aristotle Onassis

A recession is no time to embark on costly research and development projects. It is better to be ingenious about finding ways of exploiting current products. If you find one market sector closed to you, then try another. Entrepreneur Victor Kiam tells a story of how he realized that an air purifier he was selling had too many competitors in the USA and Canada, so he brought it to the UK where it is now the top seller in its field.

Become ingenious about building up your order book. Re-open contacts with all customers who might now be buying from your competitors. Your new levels of efficiency will have made you more competitive, and your commitment to quality of product and service will win you new levels of confidence from your customers.

One of the advantages of looking up old customers is that you know that they have a need of your product, and in addition you already have some contacts with the company personnel. You may have some old products you used to make for them. Why not look up the cost and the price of those products when you last made them, and then think up ways of making a better quality product for a lower price? That should interest them.

Get into the habit of seeing problems as opportunities for you to do more business. Doctors and nurses and hospitals, and businesses which supply hospitals, exist because people are sick. Industries involved in armaments, military planes, uniforms, gas masks, tents, and so on, will have had increased business opportunities during the Gulf War. Oil spillages at sea mean more demand for oil slick booms and dispersal chemicals.

In the 1991 recession, it was noticeable that travel agents had a difficult time. Yet I know one small company in Lancashire that has only been in business for about two years which survived the downturn in trade because of the work rate of the owner in paying personal attention to customer needs. Small differences in the way that customers are treated include:

- a welcome-home card waiting for holiday-makers when they return;
- a more relaxed atmosphere for people to browse through brochures in the travel agency over a cup of tea.

Trading difficulties might even become a focus of change which could revolutionize your business. They might allow you to be more bold and to push through changes which in better times would not be embraced by everyone wholeheartedly.

A prime example is the Swiss watch industry, which had 75 per cent of the world watch market until the Japanese came and took 40 per cent and other countries took another 50 per cent, leaving the Swiss watch industry with only 10 per cent. Quartz technology made it possible to combine cheapness with reliability, and the Swiss watch industry responded by reducing the number of watch parts from ninety to fifty and creating a standard watch mechanism which was adopted by a variety of Swiss companies. One company emphasized their watches as fashion accessories, with a choice of cases and straps. The Swatch, as it was called, sold a million units in its first year.

In 1980 John Brown, the UK engineering group, had £37m assets supporting £150m worth of debt, and the banks were fairly close to pulling the plug. Since then the group has gone through considerable pain to build up its resilience to a downturn. It has refashioned itself by selling off machine tools, road transport, and textile machinery companies, and taking on a partner Trafalgar House, the building contracting and shipping group. The management point to their ingenuity as their strength. For example, it built a portable power station on barges so that it can be towed around the Philippine Islands. In 1986 it cut unproductive work by more than 50 per cent and reduced lead times on gas turbines by thousands of hours. In the fabrication shop only half of the 150 workers are permanent: the rest are temporary, engaged on specific contracts. According to management, the company has 'bred a will to survive'.

Recent business history is littered with examples of how even experienced captains of industry can get it wrong. Public companies like Polly Peck, Parkfield, Hawker Siddeley, Brent Walker, and City Vision did not perform in 1991 as predicted by their chairmen. Most of the companies will survive though some, like Polly Peck, have already gone to the wall, but the lesson is that the art of survival is not the prerogative of big companies or the experienced industrialist. Your ability to react to your circumstances may well be the key to your survival.

Be tough – be persistent

When you get to the end of your rope, tie a knot and hang on.

F.D. Roosevelt

The Beatles were one of the biggest phenomena ever in pop music, yet much credit must be given to the tenacity of Brian Epstein, their manager. In 1961 he saw them in the Cellar Club in Liverpool, just another local rock-and-roll group. He became their manager, and made hundreds of phone calls, letters, and visits to recording companies to get a recording contract, but was turned down by them all. The group eventually recorded 'Love Me Do', which would have died the death except for Epstein's fierce determination. His parents' record store ordered 10 000, he wrote to the BBC and Radio Luxembourg, and visited shops all over Liverpool asking for the record. It was two years before they had a No. 1 hit, and even then ITV had to be persuaded to put them on television. Epstein went to New York to sell the Beatles, but even then 'Love Me Do' sold only a few hundred copies. Capital Records said, 'They won't do anything over here!'

Surviving is a battle – it is dangerous and uncomfortable, time-scales contract, and normal hours of work no longer apply. New rules come into operation. As Sir John Harvey-Jones said in 'The Troubleshooter', 'The cut-throat competition from overseas has never even heard of the Marquess of Queensberry Rules.'

Decisions which in good times could be delayed need to be tackled quickly. Control of debts, a reduction in total wages, inventory, and overheads, an increase in sales effort, and marketing intelligence, and improved cash flow are prerequisites. When you think about cost reduction, do not just think about cutting costs – think about eliminating them altogether. Think about doing things so differently that it wipes out whole chunks of accepted costs. Why not ask your bank to reduce interest rates, or your employees to take a 5 per cent cut in wages, or cut out discounts, even to established customers?

All the above ways of cutting costs have been achieved by companies who knew what they had to do to survive. You, too, can achieve these kinds of cost reductions if you have a clear survival plan.

Bad times will not last for ever, and if you can hang on until the upturn comes you can be in better shape to take advantage of it.

It is worth remembering this maxim from US President Coolridge: 'Press on; nothing in the world can take the place of persistence. Talent will not ... genius will not ... education will not ... ; persistence and determination alone are overwhelmingly powerful.' It is also worth remembering that, in its first year of sales, Gillette sold only fifty razors and two hundred blades!

In his book *Getting it Right the Second Time* (Mercury Books, 1991), Michael Gershman lists forty-nine business failures who faced ruin and bankruptcy before they hit the winning formulae. Companies like Kleenex and Pepsi-Cola went on to make fortunes due more to 'persistence than brilliance'.

Conclusion

There is an old saying that 'The dog that trots about finds a bone'! The game plan which you devise will only succeed if you put it into action. In a critical cash-flow situation or at a time of profit erosion, doing nothing is not an option.

Let me illustrate some of the above points with a résumé of a discussion on key business areas with the managing director of a profitable company.

Competition The company reviews the published accounts of all its competitors.
Selling They carry out a detailed analysis of the conversion rate of enquiries to orders. For example, they examine monthly every quotation sent out and they monitor each quotation monthly thereafter until it has no possibility of being converted

into an order. This requires time and effort and attention to detail.

Benefits   The price is considered as only one of the factors in winning a contract. Delivery and quality are equally important.

Commitment   The company is owned by three people who are on the premises. They work at the company and are hungry for success. These important decision-makers are available in the company almost every day to talk to customers and to 'mind the shop'.

Flexibility   The company directors acknowledge that their willingness to respond to customers and their flexibility are the main reasons why they get business.

Cost control   A key to profitability is that costs are based on an 8-hour day, even though the plant works on 16-hour or 24-hour shifts. The overhead costs are therefore recovered on a single shift working, and any double day shifts or 24-hour shifts are profitable because of the recovery of overheads.

8

A DIY PROFIT PROTECTION PROGRAMME

Nothing is particularly hard if you divide it into small jobs.
                                          Henry Ford

You will not be able to do all things well all of the time. You must therefore concentrate on the important things, the things that matter in your company: is it cost, deliveries, service, price? You will know what is right for the business you are in – make sure employees at all levels know it, too.

Having examined your company situation and knowing what you have to achieve, you now have to put the game plan into action. You have set your purpose, which becomes the destination. You now have to set some goals, which will become the routes to the destination, and you have to make it happen with your team.

Reducing costs is like trying to lose weight. The ease with which weight is put on contrasts sharply with the effort needed to shed the pounds. So it is with company costs, which in good times rise as management spends surplus money on things which are nice to do but may not be strictly necessary to the business. Such spending gets absorbed into general expenses as fixed costs of running the business, such as:

- exotic advertising;
- customer entertainment;
- executive cars;
- subsidized canteen;
- trips abroad with dubious value-for-money benefits;

- new product development;
- annual wage increases.

These are not fixed costs in the sense that they cannot be altered but, while you would not necessarily cut them out altogether, every cost must pay its way.

There should be a measure of the value of each cost centre to the business profitability. All costs should be reviewed critically, and should be budgeted and monitored. Like a weight-reducing programme, management will need to work at reducing its costs, which is not easy.

Be positive about your chances of protecting your profits. Do not believe all the tales of doom and gloom which you will read in the press, for even in a full-scale recession many companies do very well. Your game plan will make sure that you also do well.

Know your costs

You cannot control or reduce costs if you do not know what they are! Use or create cost centres – existing ones will do to begin with. Start crudely, if necessary, using existing information. Measure costs to date, and establish a base level against which you can monitor improvement.

Why do you need to know true costs?

(1) To identify areas of potential savings. A good plan is to analyze the expenditure in the profit and loss account and nominal ledger and list the spending in reducing order of value. It is likely that material, direct labour, other wages and salaries, heat, light, and power, transport, rent and rates, insurance, and so on, will each be a significant percentage of the total cost. This listing, in order of importance, will give you a clue about which cost centre to investigate.

(2) To be able to measure improvement. Without a measurement of current cost, how will you know whether to-morrow's cost is higher or lower? Or if the cost reduction programme is working?

(3)   To calculate the justification for capital spending. If you know the unit cost of a product or service, you will be able to calculate the new unit cost resulting from automation or labour-saving improvements. Then you will know the period of return of capital, or the length of time before the investment pays off.

(4)   To control cash flow. Just hoping for your debtors to pay up will not satisfy your bank manager. A clear picture of the timing of income and outgoings, determined by detailed knowledge of creditors and debtors, will give him (and you) more confidence.

(5)   To decide on alternative methods of production. Even subtle changes in working practices can make big savings. The more subtle the changes, however, the more important it is to have accurate measurement of before and after.

(6)   To stay within budget. Control means knowing where you are going. In the cost sense, this means aiming to stay within the plan of expenditure as predicted by the budget. Without up-to-date cost information, you will probably only know whether you are profitable after the auditors have been in!

How to obtain control information

The quickest way to obtain control information is to use existing sources. These might include the following.

Profit and loss account: use this to measure:

  gross profit (for product profitability);
  net profit (for management control);
  ratio of material, labour, and overheads;
  stock usage;
  stock value;
  cash-flow forecasting.

Timesheets and clock cards: for lateness/absenteeism/overtime/non-production work.

110

Stock control reports: slow moving/obsolete/value/stock outs/ turnover.

Sales ledger: debtors – who, how much, days outstanding – slow payers.

Purchase ledger: creditors – who, how much, days outstanding – most credit, biggest suppliers.

Bank statement: cash flow, ability to pay your way.

The above information exists in most companies. The better companies will also have information on the order book, capacity, performance, and profit by product, customer, and market sector.

First, use whatever control information you have, then make it more sophisticated as the need arises.

Involve heads of department

Give your cost-centre managers the job of setting targets to achieve the budget. They will respond if you give them responsibility for creating their own figures. They will 'own' them and make them work. If some managers are not capable of doing this, you have the wrong people in the job.

Profit protection is a survival game but, like a marathon runner who focuses attention on the first mile and then the second mile and then at other mile posts subsequently, you need to create short-term achievable goals. As I have suggested above, there will be some measurable quantification of progress such as increased output, reduced overheads, or lower unit costs.

Concentrate only on those actions which will help to achieve the purpose you have set yourself. Be selfish, be single-minded, create a 'tunnel vision' about your company activities.

Take the best ideas of management and staff and try to quantify the annual savings. Let people have their say about the level of improvement – it is much better that they aim to produce 10 per cent savings and only achieve 5 per cent than aim for 3 per cent and succeed. Divide the annual saving into twelve monthly periods and, if possible, divide the monthly targets into weekly ones. These short-term targets will ensure that interest is maintained in the programme.

Target to reduce costs by 1 per cent per month

If our typical company were to lose 10 per cent of its revenue yet reduced its cost by 1 per cent per month, it would end the year with more profits than before.

Do not be dismayed if lots of new ideas are not forthcoming. Just make sure that you do the things you know about really well. In any list of new ideas you are just as likely to get bad ones as in a comparable sample of old ideas. Encourage employees to come up with their own ideas on how to achieve your short-term goals. Pick out the best ideas from each group and implement them if possible. One good way of encouraging enthusiasm is to have departmental heads meet with their own staff to discuss ways of improving profit protection. On the other hand, do not encourage a great many meetings and endless discussion. Ask them to draw up a list of just three things which will improve things like cash flow, stock control, production cycle, timely deliveries, cost control, increases in productivity, or how to get more customers. You will be surprised how much they know about your business.

Create regular reports

You have to tell people. This means talking to them face to face, and explaining short-term goals to them in simple language. It might mean training or retraining people. It will mean publishing targets and publishing results frequently. Make the objectives a talking point, make the short-term goals a focus of attention among your employees.

Initially keep the target-setting and monitoring on a short time-scale. This week, next week, this month, next month, will enable you to monitor results and will give you the opportunity to make sure everyone is enthusiastic about the action.

112

Using the budgeted costs, have monthly reports generated (as a matter of routine) for all cost-centre managers. Hold monthly meetings with them and help them to achieve their own targets. Praise where possible.

Keep it simple

Use easy-to-understand cost centres, and chunky areas of cost like labour, materials, heat, light, power, transport, and so on. But do not get bogged down with detail at your level. Give your managers some freedom to do their own thing.

Never use units of measurement which are difficult for people to understand or calculate. A measurement of return on capital employed might be fine for the board of directors, but the shop-floor workers will not have the means of calculating it for themselves. Their measures should be the number of products out of the door, or a target of fewer direct hours per product, or number of items in finished goods store, or the reduction in the number of days to deliver an order.

Set them targets which depend on higher productivity, like lower labour or material or overhead costs per job. It is also essential to make the target-setting relevant to the department, such as the number of jobs through the paint shop in twenty-four hours, or the average cost of transport per product.

Most crucial of all, make sure that everyone is aware of your short-term step-by-step action plan.

Do it now

Sir John Harvey-Jones, in the book of his *Troubleshooter* television series, repeatedly talks about the need for actions to bring about desired change. He says, 'You get no rewards for intentions. Only the accomplishment counts.'

Every month that you delay cost reduction will cost you the equivalent of 8 per cent of your improved annual profits, which you will not recover. You have to earn this week's profit this week and this month's profit this month.

113

As Sir Matt Busby is reported to have said to his marvellously entertaining Manchester United Busby Babes team when he sent them out on the field: 'Do the simple thing. Do it well. Do it now.'

9

CONCLUSION

The secret of making money is to enjoy your work. If you do, nothing is hard work, no matter how many hours you put in.

Sir Billy Butlin

The successful team or individual only needs to be marginally better than the rest, and if all the words on these pages could be replaced with one password to increased profits, it would be – people.

Much has been said and written about the value of this most important company asset, and yet most managers under-use, misuse and abuse their employees' time and talent to an alarming degree. If we managed our finances like we manage our people, most companies would be insolvent.

The choice of individual techniques for cost reduction and revenue increase is not particularly important in the motivation of individuals or groups – job security, good living standards, involvement in decision-making, and a share in the company's success are what employees want.

Motivation and profitability are also about management style. Managers have a responsibility to make things happen. In a recession they have an opportunity in a participative environment to make giant steps in building a winning team. That is why the culture in a company is important: the attitude of management, the industrial relations climate, the way problems are resolved, and the common satisfaction of achieving goals are the ingredients of success. Increased profits are achievable in most companies if all employees have the same aims and are led professionally.

Surviving in difficult times requires improved discipline, a way of life aimed at self-control. The message which this book attempts to bring is that good discipline in all departments of the company will make survival more certain. Help your employees to be self-disciplined in all matters. Encourage them to protect the company – it is the source of their income, and its health determines the standard of living of all who work in it.

In times of a general trade recession it is important to remember that to everything there is a season, and that the upturn will come, eventually. Be determined to ride out the effect of the economic downturn. In all the belt-tightening, cost-cutting, and cash-saving, be attentive to the next turn of the cycle. The just-in-time philosophy adopted in industry over the past decade means that companies have no reserves of material or component stocks. When demand does increase following a downturn, the requirement for new supplies will be felt in the supply chain immediately.

One cold February morning, a snail started climbing an apple tree. As it inched upwards, a worm stuck its head out of a warm crevice to offer some advice. 'You're wasting your energy – there isn't a single apple up there.' The snail replied, 'No, but there will be by the time I arrive!'

APPENDIX: Check-list for increased profit

The following pages contain lists of the areas of cost reduction and revenue increases contained in Chapters 4 and 5. Their purpose here is to provide a convenient summary to assist management in considering which of the range of ideas suggested are likely to be fruitful in a particular company. The pages contain columns divided into increasing levels of percentage improvement in order to encourage users to make a best estimate on profit-making opportunities.

These sheets can be photocopied for distribution within the company. Senior managers can distribute them and invite their staff to participate. This will allow managers the chance to meet with all staff to explain the purpose of the lists and to encourage feedback. When we have used similar forms in conferences, workshops, and similar meetings of managers, it has been encouraging to see the level of improvements which have been identified.

Tables 5 and 6 show the results of a survey of sixty companies.

Table 5 Top five ideas where savings have been identified

Overall	% of respondents
Eliminate overtime	90
Cut stock losses	88
Make it right first time	87
Target higher productivity	87
Control unit labour costs	85

Manufacturing organizations	% of respondents
Eliminate overtime	100
Cut stock losses	100
Make it right first time	95
Buy only what you need	91
Know your costs	90

Service organizations	% of respondents
Eliminate overtime	92
Control unit labour costs	83
Target higher productivity	83
Encourage employee cost reduction	83
Buy when needed	83

Distribution and warehousing organizations	% of respondents
Pay less for goods	100
Improve methods	86
Employ better people	86
Keep good people	86
Cut stock losses	86

Table 6 Top five ideas with most potential savings

Overall	% savings
Improve cost controls	8.6
Improve methods	8.3
Target higher productivity	8.1
Employ better people	8.0
Better plant utilization	7.8

Manufacturing organizations	% savings
Improve methods	9.4
Improve cost controls	9.0
Better plant utilization	8.5
Target higher productivity	8.4
Reduce non-added-value expenses	8.4

Service organizations	% savings
Bill earlier	10.9
Collect earlier	9.3
Target higher productivity	7.5
Keep good people	6.9
Employ better people	6.9

Retailing, wholesale, distribution, warehousing organizations	% savings
Employ better people	8.0
Link pay increases to profits	7.0
Target higher productivity	7.0
Keep good people	6.3
Pay less for goods	6.3

Protect Your Profits

Cost-reduction questionnaire

Areas of cost	Potential reduction %				
	1–5	6–10	11–15	16–20	Over 20
Materials					
Buy only what you need					
Buy when needed					
Cut stock losses					
Keep up to date					
Pay less					
Products					
Know your costs					
Reduce cost through value analysis					
Make it right first time					
People					
Control unit labour cost					
Eliminate overtime					
Improve methods					
Employ better people					
Keep good people					
Target higher productivity					
Encourage employee cost reduction					

APPENDIX

Areas of cost	Potential reduction %				
	1–5	6–10	11–15	16–20	Over 20
Money					
Bill earlier					
Collect earlier					
Link pay increases to profits					
Charge for storage, etc.					
Claim all allowances					
Claim your grants					
Plant					
Better utilization					
Cost effective investment					
Shared services					
Save cost of space					
Organization					
Reduce production cycle					
Subcontract special services					
Simplify methods and systems					
Improve cost controls					
Reduce non-added-value expenses					

Protect Your Profits

Cost-reduction questionnaire

Areas of revenue	Potential revenue increase %				
	1–5	6–10	11–15	16–20	Over 20
Marketing					
Know the market-place					
How much is your product worth?					
Propose new products to existing/ new customers					
Repackage your products					
Smarter advertising					
Selling					
Set better sales targets					
'Piggy-back' selling					
Customer-sourced leads					
Bigger quantities					
Contract sales orders					
Customers					
Better customer relations					
Everyone is a potential new customer					
Pay for sales leads					
What else will customers buy?					
Your suppliers as customers					

Areas of revenue	Potential revenue increase %				
	1–5	6–10	11–15	16–20	Over 20
Pricing					
Turn more enquiries into sales					
Discounts					
Minimum order quantities					
Charge for extras					
Non-product revenue					
Asset clearance					
Rent; sublet premises					
Everyone a consultant					

BIBLIOGRAPHY

Wherever possible I have named reference books in the text but I acknowledge the contribution made by the following books to the formation of my own opinions.

Colin Barrow, *Routes to Success*, Kogan Page, 1986

Robert Bruce, *Winners*, Sidgwick & Jackson, 1986

David Clutterbuck and Sue Kernaghan, *The Phoenix Factor*, Weidenfeld & Nicolson, 1990

William Davis, *The Innovators*, Ebury Press, 1987

M. M. Gordon, *The Iococca Management Technique*, Bantam, 1987

Sir John Harvey-Jones, *The Troubleshooter*, BBC Books

Carol Kennedy, *ICI – The Company that Changed our Lives*, Century Hutchinson, 1986

Victor Kiam, *Keep Going For It*, Collins, 1988

Debbie Moore, *When a Woman Means Business*, Pavilion Books, 1990

James Pilditch, *Winning Ways*, Mercury Books, 1989

Jeffrey Robinson, *The Risk Takers – Five Years On*, Mandarin Paperbacks, 1990

Keith Smith, *The British Economic Crisis*, Penguin Books, 1989

Management Today, British Institute of Management.

INDEX

A.B. Electrolux, 59
Added Value services, 62–3
Advertising, 71–2
American working hours, 46
Apple Computers, 47
ASDA, 3
Asset clearance, 84–5
Austin Rover, 47
Avis, 45

Bankers, 97–8
Barclays Bank, 11, 41
Barth, John, 68
Bank of America, 64
B&Q, 68, 84
Beatles, The, 105
Benefit-in-kind, 31, 42
BICC, 61–2
Billing, 27–8
BIM, 9
Bonus schemes, 43–4
Bottlenecks, 56
Brecht, Bertolt, 89
Brent Walker, 104
BP, 15
British Aerospace, 2, 38
British Airways, 41
British Productivity Council, 50

British Standard 5750, 23, 79
British Steel, 41
BT, 47
Budgeting, 2, 46, 63
Busby, Sir Matt, 114
Business in the Community, 55
Butlin, Sir Billy, 115
Buying, 19–25

Caparo Industries, 2
Capital gains, 31
Carnegie, Dale, 40
Cash management, 86–94
CBI, 10, 35, 45, 61
Cecil, Lord David, 40
Change, 10
Churchill, Sir Winston, 6
City Vision, 104
Communications, 60
Company cars, 32–3, 42
Competitors, 99, 106
Consort Hotels, 55
Coolridge, President, 106
Consultancy income, 84
Controls, 8–10
Cost centres, 55, 63–4
Cost controls, 59, 91, 107
Cost reduction, 19–65, 108–14

Costing, 2, 87
County NatWest, 41
Cramphorn plc, 84
Creditors, 8
Credit control, 16–17, 33–5, 87, 91, 94–5
Customers, 80–4, 91, 97, 100–1
Customs and Excise, 30

Dale, Dr Barry, 62
Davies, Gareth, 7
Debt collection, 17, 28–9, 33–5, 42, 94–5
Deming, Dr W. Edwards, 1, 50–1
Department of Trade & Industry, 31–2
Dexion, 64
De Florian, J. P., 12
Diesel-engine cars, 33
Discipline, 116
Discounting, 77–8
Discounts, 23–4, 42
Drucker, Peter, 26, 78, 90, 95
Dunlopillo, 67

Edinburgh, Duke of, 29
Employees, 47–8, 98–9
Epstein, Brian, 105
ERF, 13
Equity income, 85
Existing customers, 81–2, 97, 100–1

Factoring, 18
Farmer, Tom, 46, 50, 101
Faster delivery, 64
Federal Express, 69
Fields, W. C., 93
Flexibility, 101–2, 107
Flynn, Errol, 26
Ford, Henry, 48
Ford Motor Co, 21

French working hours, 46

Gallup poll, 29
German working hours, 46
Gershman, Michael, 106
Grants and other Government Assistance, 31–2
Guardian, The, 41
Glynwed International, 7

Harvey-Jones, Sir John, 62, 105, 113
Hawker Siddeley, 104
Heath, Ted, 2
Heinz, H.J., 12
Heraclitus, 10
Hewlett-Packard, 21
H. Fine & Son, 83
Holliday Chemical Holdings, 54
Homebase, 68
Horton, Sir Robert, 15
Huxley, Aldous, 101

IBM, 47, 97
ICI, 3, 15, 32
Incentives, 43–5
Industrial Clothing Service, 70
Ingenious, 102–4
Inland Revenue, 28–31, 42
Inmac, 12
Interest on overdue payments, 29
Investment, 55
Invoicing, 27
Isle of Wight, 11

Jaguar Cars, 6
Japanese, 46, 50, 62, 104
Job, Steve, 47
John Brown plc, 104
Johnson, Lyndon B., President, 82
Just-In-Time, 10, 21, 60, 116

Kelloggs, 83
Key people, 42
Kiam, Victor, 70, 103
Kleenex, 106
Kwik-Fit, 46, 50, 101

Labour cost, 36–47
Lever Bros, 83
Leverhulme, Lord, 72
Lewinton, Chris, 45
Liquidity, 18, 87, 90–5
London Carriers International,
    41
Loss leader, 70
Lucas, 21, 47

Magnet Joinery, 102
Management commitment, 45,
    107, 111
Management Today, 3
Manchester Evening News, 41
Manpower required, 39
Marketing, 66–72
Marks & Spencer, 6, 58, 68
Materials, 19–25, 87
Matthews, Bernard, 72
Manchester Business School,
    100
Measurement, 11–12, 61, 89–90
Medical Insurance, 42
Methods improvement, 40
Michelin, 41
Minimum order quantities, 78–9
Money, 26–36
Montgomery, General, 99
Motivation, 37

National Adult Office, 65
National Breakdown, 69–70
National Health Service, 65
National Insurance, 29–30
National Westminster Bank, 41
New customers, 80, 82, 84

Norfrost, 23–4, 43, 89

Onassis, Aristotle, 102
Organisation, 58–65, 87
Overdue accounts, 29

P&L accounts, 6, 110
PA, 10, 45
Packaging, 70–1
Parkfield, 104
Part-time assistance, 55
Paul, St, 58
Paul, Swraj, 12
Pay, 28, 39, 41, 43, 47
PAYE, 30
Peaks and troughs, 53
People, 36–48, 86, 115–16
Pension Schemes, 42
Pepsi-Cola, 106
Peters, Tom, 5, 101
Perceived value, 68–70
Persil, 73
Phillips, 40
Piggy-back selling, 71, 73
Plant and machinery, 53–8
Plutarch, 19
Polly Peck, 104
Pricing, 68, 72–80, 95–6
Price increases, 77
Prochnon, H. V., 13
Product costing, 40, 49
Product benefits, 79, 107
Production control, 17, 60
Production cycle, 16–17, 27, 64
Productivity, 36–48
Products, 48–53
Profit, 6–12, 19, 36, 59
Profit increase check-list, 117,
    120–7
Profit Related Pay Scheme, 28
Purchase Ledger, 111
Purchasing policy, 23–4

Quality, 50–1
Quality and Reliability Year, 50
Quantum Improvement, 15–16, 61–2
Queen's Award for Industry, 79

Rank Xerox, 21
Recession Tactics, 89–107
Remington Razor, 70
Rental revenue, 58, 85
Revenue increases, 66–85
Rewards, 43–4
Rommel, General, 99
Rooney, Bill, 4
Roosevelt, F. D., 105

Sales conversions, 75, 106
Sales initiative, 70, 100–1
Sales leads, 73, 75
Sales Ledger, 111
Sales targets, 43, 47, 72
SAS Hotels, 68
Scotch Whisky Distillers, 71
Selling, 72–6, 83
Service awards, 42
Share Option Schemes, 42
Short-term improvement, 14, 91
Shrinkage, 22
Simplicity, 60–1, 113
Smith, Ernest, 69
Sony Walkman, 60
Space (cost of), 57–8
Speculation, 54–5
Spring Ram plc, 4
Standardisation, 60
Stock Control, 20–2, 16
Strategy, 13–18
Suggestion Schemes, 47
Suppliers, 24, 96
Swiss watches, 104

TACE, 15
Target setting, 14, 61–2, 112
Taxes, 7, 29–31, 42
Taylor, F. W., 53
TECs, 32
Telephone costs, 64–5
Tesco, 85
Texas, 68
Thomas Cook, 41
T.I., 45
Time, 26–7
Timesheets, 39, 110
Tolstoy, Leo, 36
Townsend, Robert, 45
Toyota, 62
Trade terms, 24, 34
Trade Unions, 7
Trafalgar House, 104
Travel Agents, 29, 103
Treasury, 58
Turnover, 35–6
Twain, Mark, 55

UMIST, 62
Up The Organisation, 45
US Car Industry, 38
Unit labour cost, 38
Utilisation, 42, 53–4, 56–7

Value Added Tax, 29–31
Value Analysis, 42, 49, 51–3
Venture Capitalists, 8

Wages and salaries, 38, 41–5, 48
Walt Disney, 102
Wickes plc, 68
Work study, 40, 51